POWER BOXING

WORKOUT
SECRETS

**A 21-Day Program to Becoming
a Devastating Knockout Puncher
in Boxing and Mixed Martial Arts**

SAMMY FRANCO

Also by Sammy Franco

Speed Boxing Secrets
Heavy Bag Training
Heavy Bag Combinations
Heavy Bag Workout
The Heavy Bag Bible
Double End Bag Training
The Complete Body Opponent Bag Book
Cane Fighting
The Widow Maker Compendium
Invincible: Mental Toughness Techniques for Peak Performance
Unleash Hell: A Step-by-Step Guide to Devastating Widow Maker Combinations
Feral Fighting: Advanced Widow Maker Fighting Techniques
The Widow Maker Program: Extreme Self-Defense for Deadly Force Situations
Savage Street Fighting: Tactical Savagery as a Last Resort
Stand and Deliver: A Street Warrior's Guide to Tactical Combat Stances
Maximum Damage: Hidden Secrets Behind Brutal Fighting Combinations
First Strike: End a Fight in Ten Seconds or Less!
The Bigger They Are, The Harder They Fall
Self-Defense Tips and Tricks
Kubotan Power: Quick & Simple Steps to Mastering the Kubotan Keychain
Gun Safety: For Home Defense and Concealed Carry
Out of the Cage: A Guide to Beating a Mixed Martial Artist on the Street
Warrior Wisdom: Inspiring Ideas from the World's Greatest Warriors
War Machine: How to Transform Yourself Into a Vicious and Deadly Street Fighter
1001 Street Fighting Secrets
When Seconds Count: Self-Defense for the Real World
Killer Instinct: Unarmed Combat for Street Survival
Street Lethal: Unarmed Urban Combat

Power Boxing Workout Secrets
Copyright © 2018 by Sammy Franco
ISBN: 978-1-941845-58-5
Printed in the United States of America

Published by Contemporary Fighting Arts, LLC.
Visit us Online at: **SammyFranco.com**

For author interviews or publicity information, please send inquiries in care of the publisher.

Contents

"Heavy Hitters are made, not born."

– Jack Dempsey

Disclaimer!

The author, publisher, and distributors of this book disclaim any liability from loss, injury, or damage, personal or otherwise, resulting from the information and procedures in this book. This book is for academic study only.

The information contained in this book is not designed to diagnose, treat, or manage any physical health conditions.

Before you begin any exercise or activity, including those suggested in this book, it is important to check with your physician to see if you have any condition that might be aggravated by strenuous training.

About Power Boxing Workout Secrets

Power Boxing Workout Secrets: A 21-Day Program to Becoming a Devastating Knockout Puncher in Boxing and Mixed Martial Arts is a unique power development program made for fighters who want to dramatically improve their power and explosiveness in a short period of time. In fact, when used correctly, this one-of-a-kind workout program will double your power in as little as 21 days.

Power Boxing Workout Secrets is different from any other boxing training program. Actually, the boxing drills and exercises featured in this book are seldom seen or discussed in boxing circles. Nevertheless, these power development "workout secrets" will allow you to quickly dominate your opponents in boxing, mixed martial arts, kick boxing and even self-defense.

With dozens of detailed photographs and easy-to-follow instructions, Power Boxing Workout Secrets has beginner, intermediate and advanced training drills and exercises that will multiply the explosiveness of your fighting skills. Best of all, this unique power enhancement program will work seamlessly with you current boxing program or combat sports workout routine.

All of information and exercises featured in this book are based on my 30+ years of research, training and teaching the fighting arts and their related disciplines. In fact, I have taught these unique skills to my top students, and I'm confident they will help you reach improved levels of power performance in the ring.

Since this is both a skill-building workbook and training guide, feel free to write in the margins, underline passages, and dog-ear the pages.

Finally, I encourage you to read this book from beginning to end, chapter by chapter. Only after you have read the entire book should you treat it as a reference and skip around, reading those chapters that directly apply to your needs.

Train hard!

Sammy Franco

Knockout Power
The Holy Grail of Boxing

Power Boxing Workout Secrets

Speed or Power?

In my best-selling book, *Speed Boxing Secrets: A 21-Day Program to Hitting Faster and Reacting Quicker in Boxing and Mixed Martial Arts*, I discussed the importance of speed performance in boxing and other combat sports.

I also stated that the two most important physical attributes of a champion boxer was speed and power. And rightfully so, both speed (the acceleration of a punch) and power (the force of a punch) do play critical roles in dominating your opponent and ultimately winning in the ring.

I further explained that speed and power are not mutually exclusive. In fact, when you apply the basic laws of kinetic energy, you'll see the two fighting attributes are directly linked to each other.

In layman terms, mass (m) times (v) velocity equals impact power. But, if you double the mass of the object (i.e., body weight) and leave the velocity (speed of the punch) constant, you will double the impact power. Furthermore, if you leave the mass of the object (i.e., body weight) constant and double the velocity (speed of the punch), you will *quadruple the power.*

Mass x Velocity = Impact Power

From this simple equation, we can derive two important conclusions:

- **Speed and Power are linked to each another.**
- **Speed is a significant power generator.**

This simple yet compelling analysis was intended to provide you with a renewed appreciation for speed performance, especially when engaged in boxing and mixed martial arts.

The truth is, speed is not an end in itself. In fact, when it's combined with power enhancement training, it creates an unbeatable combination that allows the fighter to dominate his or her sport. And that's what this book is all about.

Power Boxing Workout Secrets: A 21-Day Program to Becoming a Devastating Knockout Puncher in Boxing and Mixed Martial Arts is designed to go hand in hand with my Speed Boxing program. Like two book ends, they complement and work with each other.

Nevertheless, this Power Boxing program is a self-contained training system that produces fantastic results without the added benefit of speed performance training.

Devastating knockout power is the ultimate goal of every fighter, regardless of their sport or fighting division. Just remember, if speed is a means to an end, then knockout power is the end in itself.

The ability to unleash devastating knockout power is the ultimate goal of every boxer and mixed martial artist.

Four Reasons Fighters Want Knockout Power

There are four important reasons why every boxer should strive to develop knockout power. First, the harder you hit, the more respect your opponent will have for you in the ring. This means you are less likely to be toyed with, taunted, and tortured during a match.

Second, a power puncher is an exciting fighter. That's why boxing fans love to watch heavyweight bouts; more than in any other fighting division, there's always the greatest possibility of a sudden and spectacular knockout. Never forget that boxing and mixed martial arts is also a big business and fans expect to be entertained.

Third, bad judging is all too common in combat sports, especially boxing. However, a fighter who delivers a knockout punch controls his own fate by taking the decision making process out of the hands of the judges.

Finally, and most importantly, if you to can put a quick and decisive end to any match, you will increase your longevity in the sport. Don't forget, the longer a boxing match goes on, the greater your chances of a possible career ending injury or humiliating defeat.

Is Knockout Power a God Given Skill?

The answer to this question is both yes and no. It's true, there are only a few lucky fighters (both past and present) who naturally possess devastating punching skills. And then there's the rest of us who must train and develop it.

The good news is Power Boxing Workout Secrets breaks through the mystery of heavy hitting boxing skills. You don't have to be have the genetics of Joe Lewis, George Foreman, Jack Dempsey, or Mike Tyson to develop superhuman knockout power. You just need to know the training secrets!

Joe Louis "the Brown Bomber" is considered by many to be one of the hardest hitting boxers of all time.

When using this unique knockout development program, you'll quickly discover that smart training and a committed attitude will help you develop these devastating knockout skills.

Finally, unlike other training books, I'm not going to waste your time with mind numbing theories or bore you with pointless anecdotal stories. This book gets right to the point and teaches you exactly what you need to do to reach your performance goals.

Power Boxing Workout Secrets

Chapter 1
Power Boxing System Overview

Two Parts of Power Boxing

The Power Boxing program is a combination of two different training components that must be developed to maximize your full power potential. These Power Boxing components are:

- **Power Technique Drills:** Boxing specific drills that develop devastating knockout punching power.

- **Power Strengthening Exercises:** Specific conditioning exercises that help you unleash maximum power and explosiveness in the ring.

When you combine the power boxing drills with the strengthening exercises into a 21-day program (see Chapter 4), it creates a synergistic effect that propels your boxing skills to an entirely new level of power performance. In the final analysis, you will develop the capability to destroy anyone who is foolish enough to step into the ring with you.

When you combine the power boxing drills with the strengthening exercises, it creates a synergistic effect that takes your boxing skills to an entirely new level of power.

Boxing Fundamentals

In order to benefit from the Power Boxing drills featured in the next chapter, you must first have a solid understanding of the basic fundamentals. They include:

- **Boxing stance**
- **Boxing footwork**
- **Boxing techniques**
- **Boxing attributes**

For those of you who are new to boxing, I will briefly cover these concepts, and for those of you with a solid boxing background, please feel free to move on to the next chapter and get started.

Boxing Stance

Any coach worth his salt will agree that a boxer's ability to hit hard begins with his stance. A power puncher must first master a boxing stance that always places his feet, hips and shoulders in the proper position to deliver explosive blows.

For a right handed fighter, this means the following:

- Left side of your body faces the opponent.
- Left foot extended forward approximately a shoulder width distance from the rear foot.
- Right foot pointing toward the opponent.
- 50% weight distribution on each leg.
- Knees slightly bent.

- Torso is slightly bent.

- Both hands are up and close to your face.

- Front and rear elbows close to the body and pointing down.

- Shoulders and relaxed but ready.

- Eyes looking forward at the opponent with chin angled down.

Footwork

Footwork is an essential component of boxing because it determines your ability to move and strategically position yourself in the ring. However, many boxers don't realize that footwork also plays two important roles for delivering a knockout punch.

1. **Range Finder** - Footwork facilitates finding your range, which permits you to reach your target at the ideal distance, which will maximize the impact power of your punch.

2. **Power Amplifier** - Footwork functions as a power amplifier for your fighting techniques. Body momentum generated from footwork also acts as a power generator for your punching skills.

Boxing footwork and mobility are one and the same. I define mobility as the ability to move your body quickly and freely, which is accomplished through basic footwork. The safest footwork involves quick, economical steps performed on the balls of your feet, while you remain relaxed and balanced. Keep in mind that balance is your most important consideration.

Basic boxing footwork can be used for both offensive and defensive purposes, and it is structured around four general directions: forward, backward, right, and left.

However, always remember this footwork rule of thumb: Always move the foot closest to the direction you want to go first, and let the other foot follow an equal distance. This will always keep the feet apart from each other and prevent cross-stepping, which can cost you the fight.

Basic Footwork Movements

1. **Moving forward (forward)** - from your fighting stance, first move your front foot forward (approximately 12 inches) and then move your rear foot an equal distance.

2. **Moving backward (backward)** - from your fighting stance, first move your rear foot backward (approximately 12 inches) and then move your front foot an equal distance.

3. **Moving right (sidestep right)** - from your fighting stance, first move your right foot to the right (approximately 12 inches) and then move your left foot an equal distance.

4. **Moving left (sidestep left)** - from your fighting stance, first move your left foot to the left (approximately 12 inches) and then move your right foot an equal distance.

Practice shadowboxing with these four movements for 10 to 15 minutes a day in front of a full-length mirror. In a couple weeks, your footwork should be quick, balanced, and natural.

Circling Right and Left

Circling footwork is a slightly more advanced, where you will use your front leg as a pivot point. This type of movement can also be used defensively to evade an overwhelming combination assault or to counter strike the opponent from a strategic angle. Strategic circling can be performed from either an orthodox or southpaw stance.

1. **Circling left (from a left stance)** - this means you'll be moving your body around the ring in a clockwise direction.

From a left stance, step approximately shoulder distance to the left with your left foot. Then use your left leg as a pivot point and wheel your entire right leg to the left (in the direction of an arc) until the correct boxing stance and positioning is acquired.

2. **Circling right (from a left stance)** - this means you'll be moving your body around the ring in a counter clockwise direction. From a left stance, with your body traveling in the direction of an arc, step approximately shoulder distance to the right with your right foot, then pivot your left foot until the correct stance and positioning is acquired.

When performing circular footwork, remember the footwork rule of thumb still applies: Always move the foot closest to the direction you want to go first, and let the other foot follow an equal distance.

Boxing Techniques

Mastery of basic boxing punches is a necessity for power punching. This includes the following techniques:

- **Left Jab**
- **Straight Right**
- **Left Hook**
- **Right Hook**
- **Left Uppercut**
- **Right Uppercut**

The Jab

The jab is a foundation technique for boxers and mixed martial artists. This punch is thrown from your front hand and it has a quick snap when delivered.

1. Start off in a fighting stance with both of your hands held up in the guard position. Remember to keep both of your fists lightly clenched with both of your elbows pointing to the ground.

2. To perform the punch, simultaneously step forward and snap your front arm out.

3. Remember to turn your fist so it lands in a horizontal position.

4. When delivering the punch, remember not to lock out your arm, as this will have a "pushing effect".

5. Quickly retract your arm back to the starting position.

Straight Right

The straight right is considered the heavy artillery of punches and it's thrown from your rear arm. To execute the punch, perform the following steps:

1. Begin from the fighting stance.

2. Quickly twist your rear hips and shoulders forward as you snap your rear arm. Proper weight transfer is of paramount importance. You must shift your weight from your rear foot to your lead leg as you throw the punch.

3. Turn your fist so it lands in a horizontal position.

4. Avoid overextending the blow or exposing your chin during its execution.

5. Don't lock out your arm when throwing the punch. Let punch sink in before retracting it to the starting position.

Hook Punch

The hook is another devastating punch that's also one of the most difficult to master. This punch can be performed from either your front or rear hand and it can be thrown at both high and low targets.

To perform either the lead or rear hook punch, follow these steps:

1. Start in a fighting stance.

2. Quickly and smoothly, raise your elbow up so that your arm is parallel to the ground while simultaneously torquing your shoulder, hip, and foot into the target.

3. When delivering the punch, be certain your arm is bent at least ninety degrees and that your wrist and forearm are kept straight throughout the movement.

4. Your fist is positioned vertically and your elbow should be locked when contact is made with the opponent.

5. Return back to the starting position.

Uppercut Punch

The uppercut is a another powerful punch that can also be delivered from both the lead and rear arm. To perform the technique, follow these steps:

1. Begin from the fighting stance.

2. Next, drop your shoulder and bend your knees.

3. Quickly, lift up and drive your fist upward and into the target.

4. Your palm should be facing you when contact is made with the opponent. To avoid any possible injury, keep your wrists straight.

5. Make certain that the punch has a tight arc and that you avoid any and all "winding up" motions. A properly executed uppercut should be a tight punch and should feel like an explosive jolt.

6. Return back to the fighting stance.

Boxing Attributes

For a boxer to be effective in the ring, he or she must possess certain basic fighting attributes. Attributes are both physical and mental qualities that maximize your fighting skills.

For example, speed, power, timing, non telegraphic movement, rhythm, coordination, accuracy, balance, and mental toughness are just a few boxing attributes that must be present if any boxer is to be effective in the ring.

Let's explore a few attributes necessary for boxing: speed, power, timing, balance, and non telegraphic movement.

Speed

You need to be fast. While some athletes are blessed with great speed, the good news is that with proper training you can obtain it rather quickly. In my book Speed Boxing Secrets, I covered in great detail the importance of boxing speed training. Speed development for boxing is actually comprised of two training components:

- Visual reflexes and recognition speed
- Movement speed

Each link in the speed chain represents a particular component or micro-attribute of speed that should be trained and developed to maximize your speed performance in the ring..

Power

Power refers to the amount of impact force you can generate when hitting your opponent. Fortunately, the power of your punch is not necessarily predicated on your size and strength. A relatively small person can generate devastating knockout power if he or she follows the training principles outlined in this book.

Timing

Timing refers to your ability to execute a boxing technique at the optimum moment. There are two types of timing: defensive and offensive. Defensive timing is the time between the opponent's punch and your defensive response to that attack. Offensive timing is the time between your recognition of a target opening and your offensive response to that opening.

Balance

Effectively knockout power requires substantial follow-through while maintaining your balance. Balance is your ability to maintain equilibrium while stationary or moving. You can maintain perfect balance only through controlling your center of gravity, mastering boxing mechanics, and maintaining proper skeletal alignment.

Non Telegraphic Movement

The element of surprise is an invaluable tool in boxing. Successfully landing a knockout blow requires that you don't forewarn your opponent of your intentions. Clenching your teeth, widening your eyes, cocking your fist, and tensing your neck or shoulders are just a few common telegraphic cues that will negate the element of surprise.

One of the best ways to prevent telegraphic movement is to maintain a poker face prior to executing your punch. Make it a habit to always avoid any and all facial expressions when working out in the gym and fighting in the ring.

Chapter 2
Power Boxing Drills

Power Boxing Workout Secrets

Power Punching Goals

In this chapter, I'm going to teach you boxing specific drills that will take your power punching skills to a completely new level of performance.

These technique drills are the culmination of 30+ years of research, analysis, and experimentation in the fighting arts. I have used these power punching drills to teach many of my students, and I'm confident they will help you become a devastating fighter.

By the way, when I refer to power punching, I'm talking about explosive bone crushing impact that accomplishes one of three objectives:

- **It swiftly knocks your opponent out.**
- **It produces immediate physical damage that prevents your opponent from continuing the round.**

It causes psychological damage that impedes your opponent's ability to fight.

Punching Combinations

Most of the power boxing drills featured in this chapter will require you to perform punching combinations. For your convenience, I've provided over 50 combination examples that will benefit beginner, intermediate, and advanced fighters. Again, these are just examples of what you can use with drills in this chapter.

Beginner Combinations

1. jab-jab (all high)
2. jab-jab (all low)
3. jab-jab (high-low)

4. jab-jab (low-high)

5. jab-straight right (all high)

6. jab-straight right (high-low)

7. straight right-jab (all high)

8. jab-straight right-straight right (all high)

9. straight right-jab-straight right-jab (all high)

10. jab-jab-straight right (all high)

11. jab-jab-straight right (high-high-low)

12. jab-straight right-jab (all high)

13. jab-straight right-jab (high-low-high)

14. jab-straight right-jab-straight right (all high)

15. jab-straight right-jab-straight right (high-low-high-low)

16. jab-straight right-jab-straight right(low-high-low-high)

17. jab-straight right-jab-straight right (all low)

18. jab-jab-straight right (low-low-high)

19. jab-jab-jab (high-low-high)

Intermediate Combinations

20. jab-straight right-hook (all high)

21. jab-straight right-hook (high-high-low)

22. jab-straight right-hook-hook (all high)

23. jab-straight right-hook-hook (high-high-high-low)

24. jab-straight righthook-hook (high-high-low-high)

25. jab-rear hook-rear hook (high-high-low)

26. jab-rear hook-rear hook (high-low-high)

27. jab-lead hook-straight right (all high)

28. jab-lead hook-straight right (low-low-high)

29. jab-lead hook-rear hook (all high)

30. jab-lead hook-straight right-lead hook (all high)

31. jab-lead hook-rear hook (high-low-low)

32. jab-lead hook-rear hook (high-high-low)

33. jab-lead hook-rear hook (high-low-high)

34. jab-jab-straight right-lead hook (all high)

35. jab-jab-straight right-lead hook (high-high-high-low)

36. straight right-lead hook-lead hook-rear hook (low-high-high-low)

37. straight right-lead hook-lead hook-rear hook (high-low-low-high)

38. straight right-lead hook-straight right-lead hook-rear hook (high-high-low-high-low)

39. straight right-rear hook-rear hook-lead hook-lead hook (high-high-low-low-low)

Advanced Combinations

40. jab-jab-rear uppercut (all high)

41. jab-lead uppercut-straight right (all high)

42. jab-lead uppercut-straight right (low-high-low)

43. jab-rear uppercut-lead uppercut (all high)

44. jab-rear uppercut-lead uppercut-straight right-lead hook (all high)

45. jab-straight right-lead hook-rear uppercut (all high)

46. jab-straight right-lead hook-straight right (all high)

47. jab-straight right-lead hook-straight right-lead hook-lead hook (5x high-1 low)

48. straight right-jab-rear hook (all high)

49. straight right-jab-rear hook-lead uppercut-lead hook (high-high-low-high-high)

50. straight right-lead hook-straight right-lead hook-rear uppercut (high-high-high-low-high)

51. rear hook-lead hook-rear hook-lead uppercut (all high)

52. rear hook-lead hook-rear hook-lead hook-rear uppercut (high-low-low-low-high)

53. rear uppercut-lead uppercut-rear hook-lead hook (all high)

54. rear uppercut-lead uppercut-rear uppercut-lead uppercut (all high)

55. lead uppercut-rear uppercut-lead uppercut-rear uppercut-lead hook-lead hook-rear hook

56. rear uppercut-lead hook-rear hook-lead uppercut-lead hook (all high)

57. jab-straight right-lead & rear hooks-lead & rear uppercuts (all high)

Now, let's move on to the first power boxing drill.

Power Shadowboxing

Shadowboxing is the creative deployment of offensive and defensive boxing techniques against an imaginary opponent. It requires intense mental concentration, honest self-analysis, and a deep commitment to improving your fighting skills.

For someone on a tight budget, the good news is that shadowboxing is cheap. All you need is a full-length mirror and a place to work out. The mirror is vital. It functions as a critic, your personal boxing coach. If you're honest, the mirror will be too. It will point out every mistake - telegraphing, sloppy footwork, poor punching mechanics, and even lack of physical conditioning.

Traditional shadowboxing develops many fighting attributes like speed, balance, footwork, combination skills, sound form, and finesse. However, Power Shadowboxing differs from conventional shadowboxing because it places full emphasis on power throughout the duration of the drill.

In a nutshell, the goal of Power Shadowboxing is to throw your punches with as much force as you can muster throughout the entire round. Each punch must be delivered with maximum body torque and weight transfer. Be forewarned! Even the most experienced and conditioned boxer will find this training methodology exhausting.

As you progress, you can incorporate a weight vest, light dumbbells, or weighted boxing gloves into workouts to further enhance your power. A good Power Shadowboxing workout consists of at least three rounds lasting three minutes in duration.

You can replace boxing gloves with light dumbbells. Just remember to start out with light weights (1-3 pounds) and progressively work your way up.

Weight Vest Training

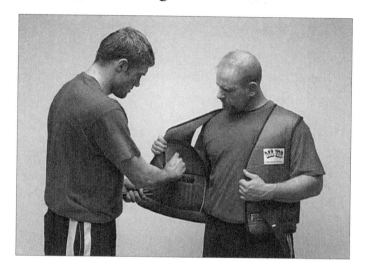

Weight vest training is another effective way to develop explosive power in the ring. By practicing your boxing skills with additional weight attached to your torso, you'll be strengthening the muscles in your body while simultaneously improving your conditioning.

Weight vest training can be incorporated into just about any boxing drill, here are just a few ways you can add it to your program:

- Shadowbox with your weight vest.
- Perform footwork drills while wearing the vest.
- Double-end bag training while wearing a vest.
- Spar with a partner while wearing a vest.
- Consider taking long walks or hikes while wearing the vest.

In order to get the best results from your workout, you'll need to invest in a high-quality vest that provides both comfort and durability. The vest must also be able to support a good deal of weight, ranging anywhere from 25-75 pounds.

A word of caution. Weight vest training is extremely demanding on your body. Be very careful when starting out. Always begin with a small amount of weight and progressively add more over time. Remember, your body needs time to adapt to the additional weight.

Be certain to speak to your doctor first to see if you have any condition that might be aggravated by this form of intense training.

Dumbbell Power Training

Dumbbell Power Training is another great way to develop knockout power by strengthening the specific muscles that are recruited when punching. This type of power boxing training allows you to focus on either a specific punch or a punching combination. It's entirely up to you.

A dumbbell workout can be structured around a prescribed number of repetitions or a period of time. They key is to perform the drill in a very slow and deliberate manner. Unlike Power Shadowboxing, your goal is to be slow and steady. Remember, throwing your punches too quickly with a lot of weight can damage your joints.

Finally, if you are going for time, strive for at least 5 rounds lasting three minutes in duration.

The jab.

The Straight right.

The lead hook.

The rear hook.

The lead uppercut.

The rear uppercut.

Resistance Punching

Resistance Punching is a very effective drill for developing both speed and power. In fact, it's also used in my Speed Boxing program for improving movement speed.

Step 1: In this demonstration, the man on the left is going to be working on his straight right. He begin by assuming a fighting stance. Next, his training partner places both of his hands over his fist.

Step 2: While maintaining the proper body mechanics, extend your punch forward. Your training partner should provide only a moderate amount of resistance.

Step 3: Continue until your punch reaches its full range of motion.

Step 4: During the retraction phase of your punch, resist your partner's forward pressure. Perform this drill for a duration of three minutes and then switch with your partner. Keep in mind, you can perform this drill with a variety of punches.

Pictured here, two students are developing the uppercut punch using the resistance drill.

Punching Mitt Power Training

The punching mitt or focus pad is an exceptional piece of training equipment. By placing the mitts at various angles and levels, the fighter can perform every conceivable punch.

Punching mitts also develops both offensive and defensive skills, accuracy, speed, target recognition, target selection, timing, and condition your entire body for boxing.

Punching mitts are constructed of durable leather designed to withstand tremendous punishment. Compared to other pieces of equipment, the mitts are relatively inexpensive. However, an effective workout requires two mitts (one for each hand).

Your training partner (called the feeder) plays a vital role in your punching mitt workout by controlling the techniques you execute and the cadence of delivery. The intensity of your workouts will depend largely upon his or her ability to manipulate the mitts and push you to your limit. I often tell my students that a good mitt feeder is one step ahead of his training partner, whereas a great mitt feeder is two steps ahead of his partner.

When training with your partner, give them constructive feedback and let them know how he or she is doing. Remember, communication is vital during your workout sessions. Also, try to avoid remaining stationary. Get into the habit of constantly moving around with quick, economical steps.

To truly benefit from any punching mitt workout, you must learn to concentrate intensely throughout the entire session. You must block out both internal and external distractions. Try to visualize the mitt as a living, breathing opponent, not an inanimate target. This type of visualization will make the difference between a poor workout and a great training session. You also might want to draw small Xs on the mitts. This practice will improve your focus and concentration and help you develop accurate striking techniques.

While the punching mitts are not traditionally used for punching power, they can still be a very effective tool. Using the mitts for power development requires you to focus exclusively on delivering power punches.

When punching the mitts, concentrate on the penetrating your target with as much force as you can muster. The goal is for every punch to be a knockout punch. Remember, however, to stay loose and relaxed at all times.

Finally, punching mitt power training is usually conducted for three minute rounds with a one minute rest. You can have your partner or coach feed you set combinations or arbitrary targets. Much of it will really depend on your skill level. If you are going for time, strive for at least 5 rounds lasting three minutes in duration.

The Gauntlet Drill

The Gauntlet drill is both a speed and power development drill. Because of its intensity, the Gauntlet drill is also a great cardio developer for fighting. To perform this challenging drill, follow these steps:

1. You'll will need a minimum of ten people, each one holding a punching mitt.

2. Divide the ten people into two equal rows and make certain they hold the punching mitt at approximately head level.

3. Next, have the designated boxer start from the top of the rows.

4. From a fighting stance, have him or her hit the mitts with a jab/straight right combination in a crisscross fashion while quickly and steadily moving down the two rows.

5. Remember to use quick footwork while staying balanced.

6. The boxer should focus exclusively on knockout power

41

punches as he works his way down the line.

7.   Once the puncher reaches the end of the "gauntlet," he runs back to the starting position (top of the row) and begins again.

8.   A good workout would be to perform this drill for 3-5 minutes non-stop.

Punch Shield Training

Punch shield training is another effective way to develop exceptional punching power. This round shield can be placed at various angles and levels, allowing you to perform every punch in your arsenal.

Like the punching mitts, your training partner plays an important role during your workout by dictating the technique and the cadence of delivery. The intensity of your workout will depend largely upon his or her ability to manipulate the shield and push you to your limit.

When training with your partner, give them constructive feedback and let them know how he or she is doing. Remember, communication is vital during your workout sessions.

When punching the shield, concentrate on the penetrating your target with as much force as you can muster. Again, the goal is for every punch to be a knockout punch.

Punch shield training is usually conducted for three minute rounds with a one minute rest. You can have your partner or coach feed you specific combinations or arbitrary targets. If you are going for time, strive for at least 5 rounds lasting three minutes in duration.

Double End Bag Power Training

There is no dispute that double end bag training is tried and true for developing both visual reflexes and movement speed in boxing. However, when used correctly, it can also be used for power training. Yes...Power training!

Double end bags are small, inflatable lightweight round bags that are most often constructed of vinyl or leather. This unique training bag is suspended in the air using two durable elastic cables that anchor it to the ceiling and the floor.

They also come in a variety of different sizes including large (9 inches), medium (7 inches) and small (6 inches). The size of the double end bag matters. The smaller the bag, the more difficult it is to hit when training.

Be forewarned! The double end bag requires a considerable amount of practice and a hell of a lot of patience. In fact, it's probably one of the most difficult pieces of boxing equipment to master.

For example, when you strike on the bag, it immediately reacts by swinging right back at you. The harder you hit the bag, the faster is rebounds. Therefore, to properly control the movement of the bag, you must strike it directly in the center. If you don't hit it dead center, it will bounce uncontrollably to the right or left.

Since double end bag training is popular in combat sports, you can find just about every type of bag variation by surfing the Internet. However, be prepared, it can be a bit overwhelming as there are so many on the market.

Once you hang the double end bag, the next important issue is making certain it is set at the proper height. One of the most common mistakes is setting the height of the bag too low. Be sure that your bag is set up so that you can effectively land head shots. Essentially, the top of the double end bag should be level with your own head.

To ensure the proper height you might have to adjust the length of the elastic rubber cables or bungee straps. This will most likely take a bit of experimentation and some trial and error, but the result will be worth the effort.

This photo demonstrates the correct height of a double-end bag. Notice how the bag is raised to a realistic target height for boxing.

It's Not Just for Speed

While the double end bag is used predominantly for visual reflexes and movement speed, it can still be a useful tool for power training. First, I recommend using a large size bag (9 inches). Compared to smaller bags, large sized double end bags tend to work better for power development.

Second, when punching the bag, you must concentrate on penetrating your target with as much force as you can muster. Each hit should be a power punch that emits a loud audible bang when contact is made. The goal is for every punch to be a knockout blow. Again, stay loose and relaxed at all times.

A good double end bag workout would consist of 5 three-minute rounds with a one minute rest period in between each round.

Larger sized double end bags tend to work better for power development.

Heavy Bag Power Training

Heavy bag training is the mother lode of power training. But, before we delve into the different heavy bag power drills, it's important to go over a few important things. For some boxers this information will be enlightening, for others it will serve as a good refresher. Regardless of your training experience, these fundamental concepts are timeless and will benefit anyone.

Benefits of Heavy Bag Training

As I discussed in my Heavy Bag Book series, the heavy bag is a fantastic piece of training equipment that provides a full range of benefits for the boxer. Some include:

- Developing and sharpening your boxing skills.
- Conditioning your entire body for the rigors of intense fighting.
- Improving muscular endurance.
- Strengthening your bones, tendons, and ligaments for the

demands of power punching.

- Conditioning your cardiovascular system.

- Relieving pent up stress.

- Channeling aggressive energy into a productive outlet.

- Developing several mental toughness attributes, such as instrumental aggression, immediate resilience, self-confidence, and attention control.

Finding the Right Heavy Bag for Power Training

For the most part, a typical heavy bag is constructed of either top grain leather, canvas or vinyl. Most bags are 14 inches in diameter and 42 inches in length. The interior of the bag is filled with either cotton fiber, thick foam, sand or other durable material. Depending on the brand, heavy bags can weigh anywhere from seventy-five to two hundred and fifty pounds.

The Heavier, The Better!

When it comes to power boxing training, the weight of the heavy bag is probably the most important consideration. As a rule of thumb, try to buy the heaviest bag you can afford. Remember, when it comes to power training, the heavier, the better!

If possible, avoid buying a bag that weighs under 100 pounds. Anything lighter won't provide sufficient resistance for knockout power development. Lighter bags tend to swing too frequently and don't permit you to fully unload the force of your punch. I personally use a 150-pound heavy bag in my power boxing program. It offers the ideal amount of resistance for intense power punching sessions.

When looking to buy a heavy bag, avoid purchasing it from your local sporting goods store, as most of these bags are cheap, poorly made, and won't provide years of reliable use. The heavy bag is a serious piece of training equipment, so you should spare no expense and look for the highest quality brand that you can afford.

The good news is you can find a reasonably priced quality bag on the Internet. Here are just a few reputable companies that stand by their products:

- **Ringside Equipment**
- **Combat Sports, Inc**
- **Title Boxing**
- **Everlast Equipment**

When it comes to power boxing training, the weight of the heavy bag is probably the most important consideration. Pictured here, a 150 pound heavy bag.

Heavy Bag Workout Gear

Before you begin working out on the heavy bag, you'll need to invest in a good pair of gloves that will protect your hands. If you don't think you'll need gloves, think again.

Striking the heavy bag (especially when power training) without hand protection causes sore knuckles, bruised bones, hand inflammation, sore wrists, and scraped knuckles. These minor injuries will set your training back for several weeks in order for your hands to heal.

Regrading hand protection, you have two options: bag gloves and boxing gloves.

Bag Gloves

Bag gloves are constructed of either top grain cowhide or durable vinyl. There are two styles of bag gloves sold on the market:

- **Mitt style gloves (recommended for boxers)**
- **Finger style gloves (recommended for mixed martial arts)**

When buying bag gloves, spare no expense and look for a high-quality brand. This will provide years of reliable use and will help ensure a better workout.

Boxing Gloves

Boxing gloves are another alternative and I strongly encourage using them when power training. Besides power development, boxing gloves are also used for developing arm strength and muscular endurance.

For power boxing training, the ideal boxing glove should have a minimum weight of 14 ounces and should also provide comfort, hand protection, and durability.

Here are some important features to look for when purchasing a pair of boxing gloves:

- To avoid wrist injuries, the glove should fit snugly.
- The boxing glove should be composed of multi-layered foam padding.
- The glove should have a sufficient palm grip that provides comfort and fist stabilization.
- To avoid a thumb injury, the glove should have thumb-lock stitching.
- The glove should be double-stitched to ensure durability.
- The entire glove should be constructed of top-quality materials to increase its durability.
- The glove should be relatively easy to slip-on and off your hands if you coach or training partner isn't around to help you put on your gloves. That's why some boxers prefer velcro fasteners over laces.

Hand Wraps

Hand Wraps or wrist wraps are used by experienced boxers who want an added measure of protection to their hands and wrists when power training on the heavy bag. They provide support to the entire hand and wrist area and can help prevent osteoarthritis in later years.

Hand wraps are long strips of cloth measuring two inches wide and nine to eighteen feet long. The longer hand wraps are more often used by boxers who have large hands and who wish to have greater hand protection. You can find hand wraps at most sporting goods stores as well as the Internet.

Hand wraps should only be used in conjunction with either large bag gloves or boxing gloves. Do not strike the heavy bag with just your hand wraps as this can easily injure your hands.

Hand wraps are washable and should be cleaned after every workout. Although there are many hand wrapping techniques, the procedures shown below is suggested.

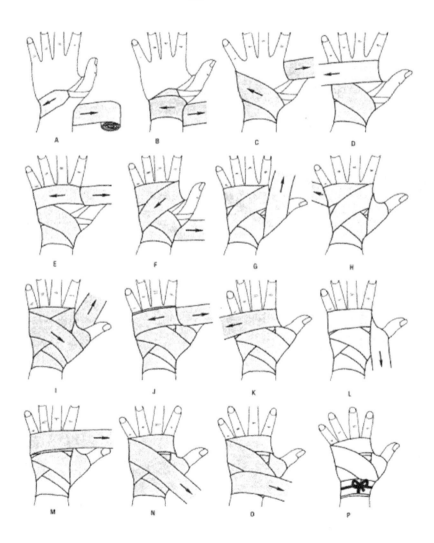

Heavy Bag Power Drills

The Elevation Drill

The elevation drill is one of the most demanding power boxing drills you can perform on the heavy bag. Besides requiring a tremendous amount of punching power and muscular endurance, the drill also requires a significant amount of mental resilience and attention control.

The objective of this exercise is to keep the heavy bag elevated at a 45-degree angle by continuously punching it. This drill is brutal on the shoulders and arms. In fact, the average boxer can barely last 30 seconds. To perform the drill follow these steps:

1. Face the heavy bag and assume a fighting stance.

2. Deliver the jab and straight right combination continuously at the bag. Concentrate on delivering full-speed, full-force punches.

3. Don't forget to use advancing footwork to assist you with your punching.

4. Maintain a rapid-fire cadence to keep the bag elevated at a 45-degree angle from the floor.

5. Avoid pushing the bag and remember to snap each punch. If the bag spins when performing this drill, it means your punches are not landing at the center of the bag. Remember to focus your blows at a single target point.

6. Perform the drill for a minimum of three rounds. Each round can last anywhere from 30 to 90 seconds. If you are exceptionally conditioned boxer, go for 90 seconds.

Elevation Drill Demonstration

Step 1: The boxer begins with a powerful jab.

Step 2: He immediately follows with straight right.

Step 3: Next, another powerful jab.

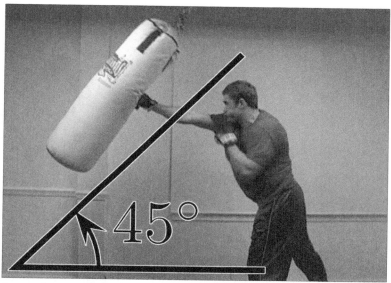

Step 4: The power of the blows should elevate the heavy bag at a 45-degree angle.

Step 5: To keep the bag elevated at 45-degrees, the boxer continues to attack the heavy bag with a barrage of full force power punches

Step 6: The boxer continues punching for a duration of 30-60 seconds.

Piston Punching

Piston Punching is another demanding power boxing drill that will push you to your limits. The objective is to fire off straight punches in a rapid-fire or piston-like fashion without elevating the bag. Piston punching can be directed to both high (head) and low (body) heavy bag targets.

Like the elevation drill, this exercise is very taxing on the shoulders and arms, so remember to take your time and gradually increase the intensity of this drill. To perform piston punching, follow these steps:

1. Face the heavy bag and assume a fighting stance.

2. Deliver the jab and straight right combination continuously on the bag. Concentrate on delivering full-speed, full-force punches.

3. Strive to hit the bag as hard as possible, throughout the entire drill.

4. Focus on snapping each punch while avoiding elevating the

bag.

5. If the bag spins when performing this drill, it means your punches are not landing at the center. Concentrate on accuracy.

6. Perform the drill for a minimum of three rounds. Each round can last anywhere from 30 to 60 seconds. If you are an exceptionally conditioned fighter, go for 90 seconds.

Piston Punching Demonstration

Step 1: The boxer squares off with the heavy bag.

Step 2: The drill begins with a powerful jab at the bag.

Step 3: Next, a straight right.

Step 4: Followed by a body jab.

Step 5: Next, a low straight right.

Step 6: Back to a high jab.

Step 7: Followed by a straight right. The drill continues for a duration of 30 to 60 seconds.

Cyclone Drill

When used correctly, the Cyclone Drill develops bone-crushing hook punches. The objective of the exercise is to assault the heavy bag with a continuous flurry of hook punches delivered in a back and forth fashion.

Like piston punching, this drill permits you to strike both high and low heavy bag targets. To perform the Cyclone drill, follow these steps:

1. Square off in front of the heavy bag and assume a fighting stance.

2. Deliver the lead and rear hook punches in a fluid, back and forth fashion. Concentrate on delivering loose and fluid full-speed hook punches in rapid motion.

3. Remember, hit the bag as hard as possible, throughout the entire drill.

4. Keep your body relaxed and remember to breathe with the cadence of your punches.

5. Work your punches up and down the bag, making certain to work both head and body targets.

6. Focus on snapping each punch and avoid elevating the heavy bag.

7. Perform the drill for a minimum of five rounds. Each round can last anywhere from 30 to 60 seconds. If you are exceptionally conditioned, go for 90 seconds

Cyclone Drill Demonstration

Step 1: The boxer assumes a stance.

Step 2: He begins with a high lead hook.

Step 3: Next, a rear hook at the bag.

Step 4: Another lead hook.

Step 5: Followed by a rear hook.

Step 6: He switches to a low body hook.

Step 7: Followed by a rear low hook. The drill continues for a duration of 30 to 60 seconds

Power Interval Drill

By now, you will come to realize that full force, full speed punching will invariably lead to a very short lived training round. In most instances, the average person can only sustain "all out" power punching for approximately 30 seconds. That's also assuming they are using proper punching form.

Any boxer worth his salt will tell you that heavy bag training is a delicate mixture of power, speed, timing, and pacing. However, the real secret to making it through a full three-minute round on the heavy bag is to pace the power of your punching.

This brings us to Power Interval heavy bag training which requires the boxer to alternate between periods of high-intensity power punching with moderate-intensity combinations.

Power Interval Workout Examples

For a typical three minute round of boxing, you can structure the Power Interval drill many different ways. Here are just two examples:

The 30/15 Interval Workout:

This is a 3 minute round that includes the following:

- 30 seconds moderate intensity
- 15 seconds high intensity power punching
- 30 seconds moderate intensity
- 15 seconds high intensity power punching
- 30 seconds moderate intensity
- 15 seconds high intensity power punching
- 30 seconds moderate intensity
- 15 seconds high intensity power punching.

The 30/30 Interval Workout:

This is a 3 minute round that includes the following:

- 30 seconds moderate intensity
- 30 seconds high intensity power punching
- 30 seconds moderate intensity
- 30 seconds high intensity power punching
- 30 seconds moderate intensity
- 30 seconds high intensity power punching.

"Punch a Hole" Drill

Unlike the previous heavy bag power drills, the "Punch a Hole" drill doesn't require you to punch the bag at a rapid fire pace. In fact, this drill actually requires you to take your time between the delivery of each and every power punch. However, there is one caveat - you must hit the bag as hard as humanly possible each and every time. Just like a highly trained military sniper, your goal is one shot, one kill.

In essence, your goal is to literally try and punch a hole through the heavy bag. Is this actually possible? I seriously doubt it. Nevertheless, this form of power training will transform your fists into sledgehammers in the ring. The Punch a Hole drill can be performed two different ways:

Technique Isolation - the boxer focuses exclusively on one punch (i.e., straight right, hook, uppercut, etc.) for the entire duration of the drill.

Combination - the boxer delivers a combination of different knockout punches for the entire duration of the drill. However, there's a perceptible delay between each punch.

The Punch a Hole drill can be performed for a prescribed number of repetitions (100 repetitions) or a predetermined period of time (3 minute rounds).

What's Next?

Now that we covered the power boxing technique drills, it's time to move on the next chapter where I will teach you the different power strengthening exercises.

Chapter 3
Power Boxing Exercises

Power Boxing Strengthening Exercises

In this chapter, I'm going to teach you power boxing strengthening exercises. The purposes of these exercises are twofold.

1. It helps **maximize power** and **explosiveness** in the ring.

2. It improves **muscular endurance** when fighting.

Power Boxing Strengthening is a combination of the following:

- **Lower body**

- **Upper body**

- **Core exercises**

Keep in mind, these exercises are not designed to serve as a full body workout or a combat conditioning program. Instead, they are used to target and condition the very same muscles that come into play when delivering a devastating knockout punch.

For reasons of simplicity, I have intentionally chosen exercises that require the least amount of gym equipment. In fact, there's a very simple workaround for those of you who don't have access to the equipment discussed in this chapter - most of the exercises can be replaced with body weight exercises.

For example, squats can be replaced with duck walks, the bench press can be swapped out for medicine ball push ups, etc.

Lower Body Exercises

The foundation of your boxing skills can be found in your stance and your legs that provide the support. Legs are also the most powerful muscle in the human body and play a critical role in power punching. Here are the most important power boxing exercises for your legs.

Squats

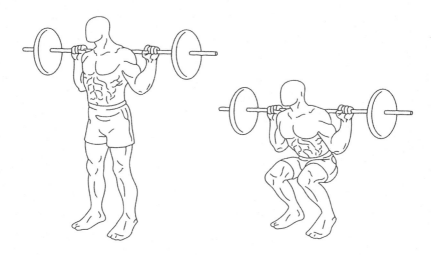

Squats are the number one weight training exercise for developing explosive leg power. This compound exercise develops the thighs, hips and buttocks. To perform the exercise, follow these steps:

1. Stand with you feet approximately shoulder width apart and in front of your hips, rest a barbell across the back of your shoulders while holding it in place with both hands.

2. While keeping your head up, back straight and your feet flush against the floor, slowly bend your knees and lower your body until your thighs are parallel to the ground.

3. Push yourself back to the starting position.

4. Perform 5 sets of 8-10 repetitions.

Deadlift

The deadlift is another compound exercise that strengthens the quadriceps, hamstrings, gluteal muscles, back, traps, and forearms. To perform the exercise, follow these steps:

1. Stand in front of an olympic bar so that your feet are approximately shoulder width apart, your toes are pointing forward.

2. Bend at the hips, lower yourself and grip the barbell with your palms facing towards you.

3. Position your hands on the bar so the are just outside of your legs.

4. Exhale and stand up with the bar.

5. With your arms straight, pull the bar up to your mid-thighs until your hips and knees are locked.

6. With you back straight, return the weight to the floor (by moving your hips back while bending your legs) in a controlled fashion.

7. Perform 4 sets of 8-10 repetitions.

Calf Raises

Calf raises are the quickest way to strengthen and develop your calf muscles. To perform the exercise, follow these steps:

1. Stand in front of a calf raise machine with your toes at the end of the footplate.

2. With your shoulders under the pads and your back straight, lower your heels as far as possible to the ground.

3. Now, lift the weight up as far as possible.

4. Slowly return to the starting position.

5. Perform 5 sets of 8-10 repetitions.

Running Bleachers/Running Stairs

Running bleachers or stairs is excellent exercise for increasing muscle mass and strength in your glutes, hamstrings, hip flexors, quadriceps and calves. Best of all, it's free and doesn't require a gym membership. All you need is a high school, college, or community center that leaves their bleachers and stadiums open to the public. For the purposes of power boxing, perform any of the following routines:

1. Sprint up the steps one at a time and quickly walk down. Repeat immediately for five total sprints.

2. Sprint up the steps two at a time and quickly walk down. Repeat immediately for five total sprints.

Bleacher Squat Jumps

If you have access to bleachers or stairs, you can also perform squat jumps. To perform the exercise, follow these steps:

1. Stand facing the stairs with your feet slightly wider than shoulder-width apart.

2. Squat down by moving your hips back and bending at your knees.

3. Load your jump by swinging your arms behind you.

4. Jump up into the air and swing your arms forward.

5. Land on the first step with your feet shoulder-width apart.

6. Quickly squat down again, swing your arms back and prepare for another jump.

7. Continue jumping up all the bleachers.

8. When you have reached the top, quickly walk down the bleachers.

9. Repeat 5 times.

Upper Body Exercises

Your upper body consists of your back, chest, shoulders, and arms. When these four muscle groups are strengthened and combined as a single deliver system for punching, the results are absolutely devastating. What follows are the best power boxing exercises for your upper body.

Pull-Ups

Pull-ups are one of the best exercises for developing upper body strength. To perform the exercise, follow these steps:

1. Grip a pull-up bar with your hands approximately shoulder width apart.

2. Your palms should be facing away from you.

3. Both of your arms should be fully extended with your body hanging above the ground.

4. Next, pull your bodyweight up until your chin is level with the bar.

5. Slowly lower yourself until your arms are back in the extended position.

6. Perform 5 sets of 8-10 repetitions.

Bench Press

The Bench Press is unmatched for developing upper body strength, including the chest, front shoulders, and triceps. To perform the exercise, follow these steps:

1. Lie on a flat bench with both of your feet flat on the floor.

2. Grab hold of the barbell (your grip should be slightly wider than shoulder width).

3. Lift the bar off the rack and slowly lower it until it touches slightly below your chest area.

4. Press the bar upward to the starting position.

5. Perform 5 sets of 8-10 repetitions.

Shoulder Press

The Shoulder Press is a
fantastic compound exercise for
developing the anterior (front)
deltoids as well as the triceps, and
traps. It can be performed while
standing of seated. To perform the
exercise, follow these steps:

1. From a seated position,
    hold two dumbbells at
    shoulder height.

2. Your grip should be
    slightly wider than
    shoulder width.

3. While keeping your back straight, press the dumbbells
    straight up to the top.

4. Slowly lower them to the starting position.

5. Repeat.

6. Perform 5 sets of 8-10 repetitions.

Core Exercises

Your core is actually comprised of many different muscles that cover the entire length of your torso which stabilize your spine and pelvis and which provide a solid foundation for explosive pivoting and torquing. Strong abdominal muscles are also important for withstanding powerful body blows.

Abdominal Crunches

Crunches are well known for strengthening the abdominal muscles as well as the obliques. When performing crunching movements, avoid interlocking your fingers behind your head. This lessens the effectiveness of the exercise and places tremendous strain on your cervical vertebrae. To perform the exercise, follow these steps:

1. Lie on your back with your feet resting on a bench with your knees bent at a 90 degree angle.

2. Cross your arms over your chest or cup your hands behind your ears.

3. In a smooth and controlled fashion, slowly lift your upper body to approximately 45-degrees from the floor

4. Then slowly lower your torso until it touches the floor.

5. Perform 4 sets of 25-50 repetitions.

Bent Knee Raise

The bent knee raise strengthens the lower abdominal region.
To perform the exercise, do the following:

1. Lie on your back with your arms stretched to your sides.

2. With your knees bent at a 60 degree angle, hold your feet off the floor.

3. Keep your back and arms down while raising your hips up and off the floor, so your knees are over your chest.

4. Contract your abdominal muscles for a second and return to the starting position.

5. Perform 4 sets of 25-50 repetitions.

Medicine Ball Waist Twist

The medicine ball waist twist is another excellent core exercise that simulates the very same twisting motion used to deliver a knockout punch. To perform the exercise, do the following:

1. Sit on the floor with both of your legs extended in front of you. Make sure both of your knees are slightly bent.

2. Hold the medicine ball with both of your hands.

3. With your elbows slightly bent, extend the ball in front of you.

4. Begin twisting your waist side to side in a slow and controlled manner.

5. Perform 4 sets of 25-50 repetitions.

The Next Step...

You are now ready to move onto chapter 4, where I will teach you how to combine the power boxing drills with the strengthening exercises into a practical 21-day program that will get you results.

Chapter 4

The 21-Day Power Boxing Workout Program

How To Create a Power Boxing Workout Program

Now we are going to take all of the knowledge from the previous chapters and put them into action. In this chapter, I'm going to teach you how to create a 21-day power boxing program. However, before we begin, you must be certain that your program meets the following criteria.

- **Realistic** - your training should be as real as possible. It should include drills and exercises that replicate the conditions of boxing.

- **Simple** - your training should be easy to put into action. It should not require time-consuming preparation or expensive or complex equipment.

- **Specific** - your training should meet specific training goals. This might be a micro goal, such as developing a power boxing technique or strengthening a specific power boxing muscle group.

- **Quantifiable** - you must be able to accurately measure your progress in training. Performance measurement is motivational and helps you stay committed to your goals. It also useful for identifying exercises that are not helping you reach your personal objectives.

Let's Get Started...

Let me start by saying, there's no single power boxing program that works for everyone. Since each of us has different goals, skill levels and timelines, it's up to you to identify your needs and personalize your training accordingly. The bottom line is, only you can determine what works best for you.

As you might imagine, there are many different ways to set up a power boxing program. In fact, some of you might want to first consult with your coach, trainer, or instructor prior to setting up a routine.

How to do it

STEP 1: IDENTIFY YOUR POWER MICRO GOAL:

For this example, let us say your goal is to specifically develop a power boxing technique, such as a knockout straight right.

STEP 2: SELECT YOUR POWER TECHNIQUE DRILLS:

Now, choose from the list of power boxing technique drills. In this case, you will choose from the 15 technique drills that are listed directly below:

Power Boxing Technique Drills:

- Power Shadowboxing
- Weight Vest Training
- Dumbbell Power Training
- Resistance Punching
- Punching Mitt Power Training
- The Gauntlet Drill
- Punch Shield Training
- Double End Bag Power Training
- The Elevation Drill
- Piston Punching
- Cyclone Drill
- Power Interval Drill: 30/15
- Power Interval Drill: 30/30
- "Punch a Hole" Drill: Technique Isolation
- "Punch a Hole" Drill: Combination

Power Boxing Strengthening Exercises:

- Squats
- Deadlift
- Calf Raises
- Running Bleachers
- Bleacher Squat Jumps
- Pull Ups
- Bench Press
- Shoulder Press
- Abdominal Crunch
- Bent Knee Raise
- Medicine Ball Waist Twist

STEP 3: DETERMINE YOUR TRAINING FREQUENCY:

Decide how many days per week you want to train. To avoid injury and prevent overtraining, refrain from power training everyday. Two or three times per week yields the best results.

STEP 4: CREATE YOUR PROGRAM:

Now that you have identified your power boxing goal, selected your power drills or exercises, and determined your training frequency, it's time to structure it around a period of one week. In this example, you will train three times per week with a micro goal of only developing a power boxing technique.

Power Boxing Workout Secrets

- **Monday** - Punching Mitt Power Training, Double End Bag Power Training
- **Tuesday** - rest
- **Wednesday** - Resistance Punching, Power Shadowboxing
- **Thursday** - rest
- **Friday** - Power Shadowboxing, Elevation Drill
- **Saturday** - rest
- **Sunday** - rest

IMPORTANT NOTE: For those of you (especially advanced fighters) who don't want to focus on a power micro goal, feel free to combine any of the power technique drills and strengthening exercises that are featured in this book.

Sample 21-Day Power Boxing Programs

What follows are sample 21-day power boxing programs. Some examples will focus on developing a power micro goal while others combine both power technique drills with strengthening exercises.

You will also find that some programs require you to train twice per week and others require three times. Again, these are just examples of what you can do. In the final analysis, it's up to you to decide what works best for you.

PROGRAM #1:

Here's a 21-day power boxing program focusing exclusively on power boxing **strengthening exercises** that requires you to train only twice per week.

Week 1

- **Monday** - Squats, Abdominal Crunch
- **Tuesday** - rest
- **Wednesday** - rest
- **Thursday** - rest
- **Friday** - Bench Press, Calf Raises, Bent Knee Raise
- **Saturday** - rest
- **Sunday** - rest

Week 2

Monday - Deadlift, Bent Knee Raise

Tuesday- rest

Wednesday- rest

Thursday - rest

Friday - Pull-Ups, Calf Raises, Medicine Ball Waist Twist

Saturday- rest

Sunday - rest

Week 3

Monday - Squats, Calf Raises, Abdominal Crunch

Tuesday - rest

Wednesday - rest

Thursday - rest

Friday - Bench Press, Pull Ups, Medicine Ball Waist Twist

Saturday - rest

Sunday - rest

PROGRAM #2:

Here's a 21-day power boxing program focusing exclusively on power boxing **strengthening exercises** that requires you to train three times per week.

Week 1

- **Monday** - Running Bleachers/Running Stairs, Abdominal Crunch
- **Tuesday** - rest
- **Wednesday** - Deadlift, Shoulder Press, Calf Raises
- **Thursday** - rest
- **Friday** - Pull Ups, Bench Press, Medicine Ball Waist Twist
- **Saturday** - rest
- **Sunday** - rest

Week 2

Monday - Squats, Abdominal Crunch

Tuesday- rest

Wednesday- Bench Press, Calf Raises

Thursday - rest

Friday - Bleacher Squat Jumps, Pull-ups

Saturday- rest

Sunday - rest

Week 3

Monday - Deadlift, Calf Raises, Abdominal Crunch

Tuesday - rest

Wednesday - Bench Press, Shoulder Press, Bent Knee Raise

Thursday - rest

Friday - Pull-Ups, Running Bleachers/Running Stairs, Medicine Ball Waist Twist

Saturday - rest

Sunday - rest

PROGRAM #3:

Here's a 21-day power boxing program focusing on power boxing **technique drills** that requires you to train only twice per week.

Week 1

- **Monday** - Power Shadowboxing, Resistance Punching
- **Tuesday** - rest
- **Wednesday** - rest
- **Thursday** - rest
- **Friday** - Weight Vest, Double End Bag Power Training
- **Saturday** - rest
- **Sunday** - rest

Week 2

- **Monday** - Dumbbell Power Training, Piston Punching
- **Tuesday** - rest
- **Wednesday** - rest
- **Thursday** - rest
- **Friday** - The Gauntlet Drill, Power Interval Drill: 30/15
- **Saturday** - rest
- **Sunday** - rest

Week 3

- **Monday** - Punch Shield, "Punch a Hole": Technique Isolation
- **Tuesday** - rest
- **Wednesday** - rest
- **Thursday** - rest
- **Friday** - Double End Bag, Power Interval Drill: 30/30
- **Saturday** - rest
- **Sunday** - rest

PROGRAM #4:

Here's a 21-day power boxing program focusing on power boxing **technique drills** that requires you to train three times per week.

Week 1

- **Monday** - Power Shadowboxing, Dumbbell Power Training
- **Tuesday** - rest
- **Wednesday** - Resistance Punching, Weight Vest Training
- **Thursday** - rest
- **Friday** - Punching Mitt Training, Power Shadowboxing
- **Saturday** - rest
- **Sunday** - rest

Week 2

- **Monday** - Power Shadowbox, "Punch a Hole": Combination
- **Tuesday** - rest
- **Wednesday** - Dumbbell Power Training, The Elevation Drill
- **Thursday** - rest
- **Friday** - Piston Punching, Cyclone Drill
- **Saturday** - rest
- **Sunday** - rest

Week 3

- **Monday** - Power Shadowboxing, Power Interval Drill: 30/15
- **Tuesday** - rest
- **Wednesday** - Double End Bag, Power Interval Drill: 30/30
- **Thursday** - rest
- **Friday** - "Punch a Hole": Technique Isolation, Cyclone Drill
- **Saturday** - rest
- **Sunday** - rest

PROGRAM #5:

Here's a 21-day power boxing program for both **strengthening exercises** and **technique drills** that requires training twice per week.

Week 1

- **Monday** - Squats, Abdominal Crunch, Power Shadowboxing
- **Tuesday** - rest
- **Wednesday** - rest
- **Thursday** - rest
- **Friday** - Pull-Ups, Bent Knee Raise, Punching Mitt Training
- **Saturday** - rest
- **Sunday** - rest

Week 2

- **Monday** - Deadlift, Abdominal Crunch, Dumbbell Training
- **Tuesday** - rest
- **Wednesday** - rest
- **Thursday** - rest
- **Friday** - Bleachers, Medicine Ball, Resistance Punching
- **Saturday** - rest
- **Sunday** - rest

Week 3

- **Monday** - Pull-Ups, Bent Knee Raise, The Elevation Drill
- **Tuesday** - rest
- **Wednesday** - rest
- **Thursday** - rest
- **Friday** - Bench Press, Abdominal Crunch, Double End Bag
- **Saturday** - rest
- **Sunday** - rest

PROGRAM #6:

Here's a 21-day power boxing program for both **strengthening exercises** and **technique drills** requiring training 3 times per week.

Week 1

- **Monday** - Squats, Calf Raises, Dumbbell Power Training, Piston Punching
- **Tuesday** - rest
- **Wednesday** - Running Bleachers/Running Stairs, Pull-Ups, Double End Bag Power Training
- **Thursday** - rest
- **Friday** - Bench Press, Medicine Ball Waist Twist, The Elevation Drill, Punch Shield Training
- **Saturday** - rest
- **Sunday** - rest

Week 2

- **Monday** - Deadlift, Abdominal Crunch, Power Shadowboxing, Resistance Punching
- **Tuesday** - rest
- **Wednesday** - Shoulder Press, Calf Raises, Punching Mitt Power Training
- **Thursday** - rest
- **Friday** - Running Bleachers/Running Stairs, Bleacher Squat Jumps, "Punch a Hole" Drill: Technique Isolation
- **Saturday** - rest
- **Sunday** - rest

Week 3

- **Monday** - Squats, Pull-Ups, Power Interval Drill: 30/30
- **Tuesday** - rest
- **Wednesday** - Bench Press, Shoulder Press, "Punch a Hole" Drill: Combination
- **Thursday** - rest
- **Friday** - Bleacher Squat Jumps, Abdominal Crunch, Medicine Ball Waist Twist, Double End Bag Power Training
- **Saturday** - rest
- **Sunday** - rest

Finding the Right Training Partner

As I discussed earlier, many of these exercises can be performed individually, while others will require the assistance of a training partner, instructor or coach.

A good training partner should motivate, challenge and push you to your limits. He or she doesn't have to share the same goals as you do, but they must be willing to help you reach your full potential. Your training partner or coach should also be somewhat familiar with the various power drills and equipment. For example, they should know how to hold and manipulate the focus mitts or perform full-contact exercises.

While a good training partner can be a major asset, having a bad one can be a major liability. Be exceptionally careful who you choose to train with you. When looking for a training parter, try to avoid the following personality types:

The conversationalist - someone who talks too much and often disrupts the training intensity.

The challenger - someone who is naturally argumentative and tries to test your knowledge and patience.

The ego tripper - someone who will do anything to prove just how tough he is. He usually enjoys full-contact drills and likes to injure others in training.

The insecure one - someone who is hesitant to participate in training full-contact drills and exercises.

The know-it-all - someone who thinks he knows anything and everything about boxing.

The dilettante - someone who doesn't understand the importance of power training, and therefore doesn't fully commit himself to the program.

Finally, remember that a good training partner or coach is there to evaluate your performance during your workouts. Listen carefully to what he has to say. A good coach, for example, will be brutally honest and tell you what you are doing correctly and what you are doing wrong. Learn to put your ego aside and heed his advice.

Safety When Training

Safety precautions must always be taken when engaged in power training. Remember, a serious injury can set you back for weeks and even months. Don't make the mistake of letting your ego or laziness get the best of you. Learn to be safety-conscious. Here are a few suggestions to help minimize the possibilities of injury when training:

- Buy the best boxing equipment that you can afford.

- Know the proper way to use training equipment.

- Regularly inspect your equipment for wear and defects.

- Avoid ego-driven training partners or coaches.

- Be especially aware when training with someone of superior power, skill, or experience.

- Always warm up before training.

- Drink plenty of water during training sessions to avoid dehydration.

- Be cautious when performing training drills for the first time.

It's also a good idea to have a first-aid kit nearby. A first-aid kit is intended for both minor and major injuries. The kit should be kept in a well-sealed box away from children. Don't forget to write down the emergency number for your local hospital or medical clinic on the box. Most first-aid kits can be purchased at your local drugstore. Each kit should contain cotton wool and hydrogen peroxide for cleaning cuts, tweezers, scissors, triangular bandages, alcohol swabs, adhesive tape, adhesive bandages, antibiotic ointment, sterile pads, gauze bandages, and elastic bandages for sprains and for elbow and knee injuries.

Avoiding Overtraining & Burnout

Burnout is defined as a negative emotional state acquired by physical overtraining. Some symptoms of burnout include physical illness, boredom, anxiety, disinterest in training, and general sluggish behavior. Whether you are a beginner or expert, you're susceptible to burnout. Here are a few suggestions to help avoid burnout in your training:

- Make your workouts intense but enjoyable.

- Vary your training routine (i.e., hard day/easy day routine).

- Power train to different types of music.

- Pace yourself during your workouts - don't try to do it all in one day.

- Listen to your body- if you don't feel up to training, skip a day.

- Work out in different types of environments.

- Use different types of training equipment.

- Workout with different training partners.

- Keep accurate records of your training routine.

- Vary the intensity of your training throughout your workout.

Keeping Track of Your Power Training

In order to reap the full benefits of training, you need to keep track of your workouts and monitor your progress. Monitoring your training will give you a wide range of benefits, including:

1. Help determine if you making progress in your training.

2. The ability to effectively alter your training program.

3. Track your rate of progress.

4. Stay interested and motivated.

5. Break through power performance plateaus.

Two of the best tools for keeping track of your training progress are: the training journal and video footage. Let's take a look at each one.

The Training Journal

Record keeping is one of the most important and often neglected aspects of power boxing training. Try to make it a habit to keep accurate records of your workouts in a personal journal. This type of record keeping is important for some of the following reasons:

1. It will help you monitor your progress.

2. It will keep you organized.

3. It will inspire, motivate and remind you to stick to your goals.

4. It helps prevent potential injuries.

5. It will help you guard against over training.

6. If you are learning new skills, it accelerates the learning process.

7. It gives you valuable training information that can be analyzed.

8. It helps you determine which power drills and exercises are unproductive.

9. It helps you determine which activities are helpful and productive.

When making entries into your journal, don't forget to include some of the following important details:

- The date and time you trained.

- The power drill or exercise you are training.

- The types of power drills or exercises you performed.

- The number or sets, reps you performed for each exercise or drill.

- The number or rounds and minutes per round you performed for each drill or exercise.

- The feelings you experienced before, during, and after your workout.

- Your overall mood.

- Concerns you have about your current training.

- Comments, ideas and observations made by your coach, training partner or instructor.

Videotaping Your Workouts

If you really want to actually see your progress, videotape your workouts. The video will provide you with a more accurate picture of what you are doing in your training. You will be able to observe mistakes and recognize your strengths and weaknesses. The video footage will also motivate you to train harder. Remember to date each videotape or video clip; later on you will be able to compare and see marked improvements in your power performance.

Chapter 5
Bonus Power Boxing Training Material

Bonus Training Material

I have included this bonus material for those of you who would like to add additional exercises into your Power Boxing program. If you have the time, these additional exercises can be incorporated with your 21-Day routine or they can be performed at your leisure. It's entirely up to you or the sage advice of your boxing coach.

Injury Free Power Punching Tips

Since we are talking developing devastating punching power, it's essential that you know how to avoid sustaining a hand injury. Essentially, this requires you to have an understanding of a few concepts and principles.

What Causes Hand Injuries?

There are four main causes of punching related hand injuries. They are incorrect fist configuration, skeletal misalignment, weak hands, wrist and forearms and hitting the wrong anatomical target.

While there are different body mechanics for each and every punch in boxing, there are four things you must know in order to avoid a hand injury, especially when power punching. They are:

- How to make a proper fist.
- Possessing strong hands, wrists, and forearms.
- Maintaining skeletal alignment when punching.
- Pinpoint target accuracy.

How to Make a Proper Fist

It's ironic that some of the most experienced boxers and MMA fighters don't really know how to make a proper fist. As you can imagine, improper fist clenching can be disastrous when power punching (especially when training on the heavy bag). Here are some possible injuries that can occur:

- Jammed, sprained, or broken fingers.

- Sprained or broken wrist.

- Significant power loss.

To make a proper fist, make sure your fingers are tightly clenched and that your thumb is securely wrapped around your second and third knuckles. Your fist should resemble a solid brick. Remember, if you cannot make a proper fist, you will not be capable of delivering a solid power punch!

You Must Keep Everything Straight

Now that you know how to make a proper fist, your next step is learning how to maintaining skeletal alignment when your fist makes contact with the target. Skeletal alignment will help ensure that both your hand and wrists will not buckle and break during impact.

Center Glove Contact

In order to maintain skeletal alignment when power punching, you need to always hit with the center of your glove. This is important because it affords proper alignment and maximizes the impact of your blow.

Center glove contact also prevents a broken hand or "boxer's fracture" from occurring. Essentially, a boxer's fracture occurs when the small metacarpal bone bends downward and toward the palm of the hand during impact with an extremely hard surface.

Wrist and Forearm Alignment

If you want to avoid breaking or spraining your wrists, you must always remember to keep your wrists aligned with your forearm throughout the execution of your punch. This applies to both straight and circular punches.

If your wrist bends or collapses on impact, you will either sprain or break it. It's that simple. Remember, all it takes is a sprained or broken wrist to end the match.

Also, don't make the false assumption that boxing gloves or hands wraps will always keep your wrists straight. I know of several boxers who actually sprained their wrists while wearing both hand wraps and boxing gloves.

Ironically, one of the best ways to learn how to throw a injury free knockout punches is to regularly workout on the heavy bag. Regular heavy bag training will provide the necessary amount of resistance to progressively strengthen and condition the bones, tendons and ligaments in your wrists.

Strong Hands, Wrists and Forearms

Proper fist configuration and wrist alignment is only half of the equation. You must also have strong hands, wrists, and forearms that can withstand the force of power punching.

What follows are several efficient ways to strengthen your hands, wrists and forearms for the rigors of power punching.

Conditioning and Strength Training

Tennis Ball

If you are low on cash and just starting out with your training, you can begin by squeezing a tennis ball a couple times per week. One hundred repetitions per hand would be a great start. You can also perform a "time hold" workout where you would hold your squeeze fo approximately five to ten seconds, and then slowly release the pressure. You would repeat this process anywhere from 10 to 15 repetitions. Next, switch the ball to your other hand and start over.

Power Putty

One excellent hand exerciser that strengthens all the muscles in your fingers and hands is Power Putty. Essentially, Power Putty is a flexible silicone rubber that can be squeezed, stretched, and crushed. Begin using the putty for ten minute sessions and progressively build up to thirty minutes. This tough resistant putty will strengthen the muscles of your forearm, wrists, hands and fingers. Remember to work both hands equally.

Hand Grippers

Another effective way to strengthen your hands, wrists and forearms is to work out with heavy duty hand grippers. While there are a wide selection of them on the market, I personally prefer using the Captains of Crush brand. These high quality grippers are virtually indestructible and they are sold in a variety of different resistance levels ranging from 60 to 365 pounds.

Weight Training

Finally, you can also strengthen your wrists and forearms by performing various forearm exercises with free weights. Exercises like: hammer curls, reverse curls, wrist curls, and reverse wrist curls are great for developing powerful forearms. When training your forearms, be certain to work both your extensor and flexor muscles. Let's look at some of the exercises.

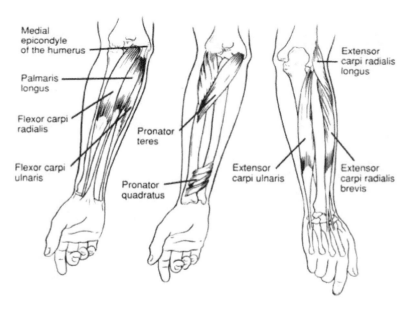

Barbell Wrist Curls

This exercise strengthens the flexor muscles. Perform 5 sets of 8-10 repetitions. To perform the exercise, follow these steps:

1. Sit at the end of a bench, grab a barbell with an underhand grip and place both of your hands close together.

2. In a smooth and controlled fashion, slowly bend your wrists and lower the barbell toward the floor.

111

3. Contract your forearms and curl the weight back to the starting position.

Reverse Wrist Curls

This exercise develops and strengthens the extensor muscle of the forearm. Perform 6 sets of 6-8 repetitions. To perform the exercise, follow these steps:

1. Sit at the end of a bench, hold a barbell with an overhand grip (your hands should be approximately 11 inches apart) and place your forearms on top of your thighs.

2. Slowly lower the barbell as far as your wrists will allow.

3. Flex your wrists upward back to the starting position.

Behind-the-Back Wrist Curls

This exercise strengthens both the flexor muscles of the forearms. Perform 5 sets of 6-8 repetitions To perform the exercise, follow these steps:

1. Hold a barbell behind your back at arm's length (your hands should be approximately shoulder-width apart).

2. Uncurl your finger and let the barbell slowly roll down your palms.

3. Close your hands and roll the barbell back into your hands.

Hammer Curls

This exercise strengthens both the Brachialis and Brachioradialis muscles. Perform 5 sets of 8-10 repetitions. To perform the exercise, follow these steps:

1. Stand with both feet approximately shoulder width apart, with both dumbbells at your sides.

2. Keeping your elbows close to your body and your palms facing inward, slowly curl both dumbbells upward towards your shoulders.

3. Slowly return to the starting position.

Reverse Barbell Curls

Reverse curls can be a great alternative to hammer curls. This exercise strengthens both the Brachialis and Brachioradialis muscles. Perform 5 sets of 8-10 repetitions. To perform the exercise, follow these steps:

1. Stand with both feet approximately shoulder width apart. Hold a barbell with your palms facing down (pronated grip).

2. Keeping your upper arms stationary, curl the weights up until the bar is at shoulder level.

3. Slowly return to the starting position.

Glossary

A

accuracy—The precise or exact projection of force. Accuracy is also defined as the ability to execute a combative movement with precision and exactness.

adaptability—The ability to physically and psychologically adjust to new or different conditions or circumstances of combat.

advanced first-strike tools—Offensive techniques that are specifically used when confronted with multiple opponents.

aerobic exercise—Literally, "with air." Exercise that elevates the heart rate to a training level for a prolonged period of time, usually 30 minutes.

affective preparedness – One of the three components of preparedness. Affective preparedness means being emotionally, philosophically, and spiritually prepared for the strains of combat. See cognitive preparedness and psychomotor preparedness.

aggression—Hostile and injurious behavior directed toward a person.

aggressive response—One of the three possible counters when assaulted by a grab, choke, or hold from a standing position. Aggressive response requires you to counter the enemy with destructive blows and strikes. See moderate response and passive response.

aggressive hand positioning—Placement of hands so as to imply aggressive or hostile intentions.

agility—An attribute of combat. One's ability to move his or her body quickly and gracefully.

amalgamation—A scientific process of uniting or merging.

ambidextrous—The ability to perform with equal facility on both the right and left sides of the body.

anabolic steroids – synthetic chemical compounds that resemble the male sex hormone testosterone. This performance-enhancing drug is known to increase lean muscle mass, strength, and endurance.

analysis and integration—One of the five elements of CFA's mental component. This is the painstaking process of breaking down various elements, concepts, sciences, and disciplines into their atomic parts, and then methodically and strategically analyzing, experimenting, and drastically modifying the information so that it fulfills three combative requirements: efficiency, effectiveness, and safety. Only then is it finally integrated into the CFA system.

anatomical striking targets—The various anatomical body targets that can be struck and which are especially vulnerable to potential harm. They include: the eyes, temple, nose, chin, back of neck, front of neck, solar plexus, ribs, groin, thighs, knees, shins, and instep.

anchoring – The strategic process of trapping the assailant's neck or limb in order to control the range of engagement during razing.

assailant—A person who threatens or attacks another person.

assault—The threat or willful attempt to inflict injury upon the person of another.

assault and battery—The unlawful touching of another person without justification.

assessment—The process of rapidly gathering, analyzing, and accurately evaluating information in terms of threat and danger. You can assess people, places, actions, and objects.

attack—Offensive action designed to physically control, injure, or kill another person.

attack by combination (ABC) - One of the five methods of attack. See compound attack.

attack by drawing (ABD) - One of the five methods of attack. A method of attack predicated on counterattack.

attitude—One of the three factors that determine who wins a street fight. Attitude means being emotionally, philosophically, and spiritually liberated from societal and religious mores. See skills and knowledge.

attributes of combat—The physical, mental, and spiritual qualities that enhance combat skills and tactics.

awareness—Perception or knowledge of people, places, actions, and objects. (In CFA, there are three categories of tactical awareness: criminal awareness, situational awareness, and self-awareness.)

B

balance—One's ability to maintain equilibrium while stationary or moving.

blading the body—Strategically positioning your body at a 45-degree angle.

blitz and disengage—A style of sparring whereby a fighter moves into a range of combat, unleashes a strategic compound attack, and then quickly disengages to a safe distance. Of all sparring methodologies, the blitz and disengage most closely resembles a real street fight.

block—A defensive tool designed to intercept the assailant's attack by placing a non-vital target between the assailant's strike and your vital body target.

body composition—The ratio of fat to lean body tissue.

body language—Nonverbal communication through posture,

gestures, and facial expressions.

body mechanics—Technically precise body movement during the execution of a body weapon, defensive technique, or other fighting maneuver.

body tackle – A tackle that occurs when your opponent haphazardly rushes forward and plows his body into yours.

body weapon—Also known as a tool, one of the various body parts that can be used to strike or otherwise injure or kill a criminal assailant.

burn out—A negative emotional state acquired by physically over- training. Some symptoms include: illness, boredom, anxiety, disinterest in training, and general sluggishness.

C

cadence—Coordinating tempo and rhythm to establish a timing pattern of movement.

cardiorespiratory conditioning—The component of physical fitness that deals with the heart, lungs, and circulatory system.

centerline—An imaginary vertical line that divides your body in half and which contains many of your vital anatomical targets.

choke holds—Holds that impair the flow of blood or oxygen to the brain.

circular movements—Movements that follow the direction of a curve.

close-quarter combat—One of the three ranges of knife and bludgeon combat. At this distance, you can strike, slash, or stab your assailant with a variety of close-quarter techniques.

cognitive development—One of the five elements of CFA's mental component. The process of developing and enhancing your fighting skills through specific mental exercises and techniques. See analysis and integration, killer instinct, philosophy, and strategic/tactical development.

cognitive exercises—Various mental exercises used to enhance fighting skills and tactics.

cognitive preparedness – One of the three components of preparedness. Cognitive preparedness means being equipped with the strategic concepts, principles, and general knowledge of combat. See affective preparedness and psychomotor preparedness.

combat-oriented training—Training that is specifically related to the harsh realities of both armed and unarmed combat. See ritual-oriented training and sport-oriented training.

combative arts—The various arts of war. See martial arts.

combative attributes—See attributes of combat.

combative fitness—A state characterized by cardiorespiratory and muscular/skeletal conditioning, as well as proper body composition.

combative mentality—Also known as the killer instinct, this is a combative state of mind necessary for fighting. See killer instinct.

combat ranges—The various ranges of unarmed combat.

combative utility—The quality of condition of being combatively useful.

combination(s)—See compound attack.

common peroneal nerve—A pressure point area located approximately four to six inches above the knee on the midline of the outside of the thigh.

composure—A combative attribute. Composure is a quiet and focused mind-set that enables you to acquire your combative agenda.

compound attack—One of the five conventional methods of attack. Two or more body weapons launched in strategic succession whereby the fighter overwhelms his assailant with a flurry of full speed, full-force blows.

conditioning training—A CFA training methodology requiring the practitioner to deliver a variety of offensive and defensive combinations for a 4-minute period. See proficiency training and street training.

contact evasion—Physically moving or manipulating your body to avoid being tackled by the adversary.

Contemporary Fighting Arts—A modern martial art and self-defense system made up of three parts: physical, mental, and spiritual.

conventional ground-fighting tools—Specific ground-fighting techniques designed to control, restrain, and temporarily incapacitate your adversary. Some conventional ground fighting tactics include: submission holds, locks, certain choking techniques, and specific striking techniques.

coordination—A physical attribute characterized by the ability to perform a technique or movement with efficiency, balance, and accuracy.

counterattack—Offensive action made to counter an assailant's initial attack.

courage—A combative attribute. The state of mind and spirit that enables a fighter to face danger and vicissitudes with confidence, resolution, and bravery.

creatine monohydrate—A tasteless and odorless white powder that mimics some of the effects of anabolic steroids. Creatine is a safe body-building product that can benefit anyone who wants to increase their strength, endurance, and lean muscle mass.

criminal awareness—One of the three categories of CFA awareness. It involves a general understanding and knowledge of the nature and dynamics of a criminal's motivations, mentalities, methods, and capabilities to perpetrate violent crime. See situational awareness and self-awareness.

criminal justice—The study of criminal law and the procedures associated with its enforcement.

criminology—The scientific study of crime and criminals.

cross-stepping—The process of crossing one foot in front of or behind the other when moving.

crushing tactics—Nuclear grappling-range techniques designed to crush the assailant's anatomical targets.

D

deadly force—Weapons or techniques that may result in unconsciousness, permanent disfigurement, or death.

deception—A combative attribute. A stratagem whereby you delude your assailant.

decisiveness—A combative attribute. The ability to follow a tactical course of action that is unwavering and focused.

defense—The ability to strategically thwart an assailant's attack (armed or unarmed).

defensive flow—A progression of continuous defensive responses.

defensive mentality—A defensive mind-set.

defensive reaction time—The elapsed time between an assailant's physical attack and your defensive response to that attack. See offensive reaction time.

demeanor—A person's outward behavior. One of the essential

factors to consider when assessing a threatening individual.

diet—A lifestyle of healthy eating.

disingenuous vocalization—The strategic and deceptive utilization of words to successfully launch a preemptive strike at your adversary.

distancing—The ability to quickly understand spatial relationships and how they relate to combat.

distractionary tactics—Various verbal and physical tactics designed to distract your adversary.

double-end bag—A small leather ball hung from the ceiling and anchored to the floor with bungee cord. It helps develop striking accuracy, speed, timing, eye-hand coordination, footwork and overall defensive skills.

double-leg takedown—A takedown that occurs when your opponent shoots for both of your legs to force you to the ground.

E

ectomorph—One of the three somatotypes. A body type characterized by a high degree of slenderness, angularity, and fragility. See endomorph and mesomorph.

effectiveness—One of the three criteria for a CFA body weapon, technique, tactic, or maneuver. It means the ability to produce a desired effect. See efficiency and safety.

efficiency—One of the three criteria for a CFA body weapon, technique, tactic, or maneuver. It means the ability to reach an objective quickly and economically. See effectiveness and safety.

emotionless—A combative attribute. Being temporarily devoid of human feeling.

endomorph—One of the three somatotypes. A body type characterized by a high degree of roundness, softness, and body fat. See ectomorph and mesomorph.

evasion—A defensive maneuver that allows you to strategically maneuver your body away from the assailant's strike.

evasive sidestepping—Evasive footwork where the practitioner moves to either the right or left side.

evasiveness—A combative attribute. The ability to avoid threat or danger.

excessive force—An amount of force that exceeds the need for a particular event and is unjustified in the eyes of the law.

experimentation—The painstaking process of testing a combative hypothesis or theory.

explosiveness—A combative attribute that is characterized by a sudden outburst of violent energy.

F

fear—A strong and unpleasant emotion caused by the anticipation or awareness of threat or danger. There are three stages of fear in order of intensity: fright, panic, and terror. See fright, panic, and terror.

feeder—A skilled technician who manipulates the focus mitts.

femoral nerve—A pressure point area located approximately 6 inches above the knee on the inside of the thigh.

fighting stance—Any one of the stances used in CFA's system. A strategic posture you can assume when face-to-face with an unarmed assailant(s). The fighting stance is generally used after you have launched your first-strike tool.

fight-or-flight syndrome—A response of the sympathetic nervous system to a fearful and threatening situation, during which it prepares your body to either fight or flee from the perceived danger.

finesse—A combative attribute. The ability to skillfully execute a movement or a series of movements with grace and refinement.

first strike—Proactive force used to interrupt the initial stages of an assault before it becomes a self-defense situation.

first-strike principle—A CFA principle that states that when physical danger is imminent and you have no other tactical option but to fight back, you should strike first, strike fast, and strike with authority and keep the pressure on.

first-strike stance—One of the stances used in CFA's system. A strategic posture used prior to initiating a first strike.

first-strike tools—Specific offensive tools designed to initiate a preemptive strike against your adversary.

fisted blows – Hand blows delivered with a clenched fist.

five tactical options – The five strategic responses you can make in a self-defense situation, listed in order of increasing level of resistance: comply, escape, de-escalate, assert, and fight back.

flexibility—The muscles' ability to move through maximum natural ranges. See muscular/skeletal conditioning.

focus mitts—Durable leather hand mitts used to develop and sharpen offensive and defensive skills.

footwork—Quick, economical steps performed on the balls of the feet while you are relaxed, alert, and balanced. Footwork is structured around four general movements: forward, backward, right, and left.

fractal tool—Offensive or defensive tools that can be used in more than one combat range.

fright—The first stage of fear; quick and sudden fear. See panic and terror.

full Beat – One of the four beat classifications in the Widow Maker Program. The full beat strike has a complete initiation and retraction phase.

G

going postal - a slang term referring to a person who suddenly and unexpectedly attacks you with an explosive and frenzied flurry of blows. Also known as postal attack.

grappling range—One of the three ranges of unarmed combat. Grappling range is the closest distance of unarmed combat from which you can employ a wide variety of close-quarter tools and techniques. The grappling range of unarmed combat is also divided into two planes: vertical (standing) and horizontal (ground fighting). See kicking range and punching range.

grappling-range tools—The various body tools and techniques that are employed in the grappling range of unarmed combat, including head butts; biting, tearing, clawing, crushing, and gouging tactics; foot stomps, horizontal, vertical, and diagonal elbow strikes, vertical and diagonal knee strikes, chokes, strangles, joint locks, and holds. See punching range tools and kicking range tools.

ground fighting—Also known as the horizontal grappling plane, this is fighting that takes place on the ground.

guard—Also known as the hand guard, this refers to a fighter's hand positioning.

guard position—Also known as leg guard or scissors hold, this is a ground-fighting position in which a fighter is on his back holding his opponent between his legs.

H

half beat – One of the four beat classifications in the Widow

Maker Program. The half beat strike is delivered through the retraction phase of the proceeding strike.

hand immobilization attack (HIA) - One of the five methods of attack. A method of attack whereby the practitioner traps his opponent's limb or limbs in order to execute an offense attack of his own.

hand positioning—See guard.

hand wraps—Long strips of cotton that are wrapped around the hands and wrists for greater protection.

haymaker—A wild and telegraphed swing of the arms executed by an unskilled fighter.

head-hunter—A fighter who primarily attacks the head.

heavy bag—A large cylindrical bag used to develop kicking, punching, or striking power.

high-line kick—One of the two different classifications of a kick. A kick that is directed to targets above an assailant's waist level. See low-line kick.

hip fusing—A full-contact drill that teaches a fighter to "stand his ground" and overcome the fear of exchanging blows with a stronger opponent. This exercise is performed by connecting two fighters with a 3-foot chain, forcing them to fight in the punching range of unarmed combat.

histrionics—The field of theatrics or acting.

hook kick—A circular kick that can be delivered in both kicking and punching ranges.

hook punch—A circular punch that can be delivered in both the punching and grappling ranges.

I

impact power—Destructive force generated by mass and velocity.

impact training—A training exercise that develops pain tolerance.

incapacitate—To disable an assailant by rendering him unconscious or damaging his bones, joints, or organs.

initiative—Making the first offensive move in combat.

inside position—The area between the opponent's arms, where he has the greatest amount of control.

intent—One of the essential factors to consider when assessing a threatening individual. The assailant's purpose or motive. See demeanor, positioning, range, and weapon capability.

intuition—The innate ability to know or sense something without the use of rational thought.

J

jeet kune do (JKD) - "Way of the intercepting fist." Bruce Lee's approach to the martial arts, which includes his innovative concepts, theories, methodologies, and philosophies.

jersey Pull – Strategically pulling the assailant's shirt or jacket over his head as he disengages from the clinch position.

joint lock—A grappling-range technique that immobilizes the assailant's joint.

K

kick—A sudden, forceful strike with the foot.

kicking range—One of the three ranges of unarmed combat. Kicking range is the furthest distance of unarmed combat wherein you use your legs to strike an assailant. See grappling range and punching range.

kicking-range tools—The various body weapons employed in the kicking range of unarmed combat, including side kicks, push kicks, hook kicks, and vertical kicks.

killer instinct—A cold, primal mentality that surges to your consciousness and turns you into a vicious fighter.

kinesics—The study of nonlinguistic body movement communications. (For example, eye movement, shrugs, or facial gestures.)

kinesiology—The study of principles and mechanics of human movement.

kinesthetic perception—The ability to accurately feel your body during the execution of a particular movement.

knowledge—One of the three factors that determine who will win a street fight. Knowledge means knowing and understanding how to fight. See skills and attitude.

L

lead side -The side of the body that faces an assailant.

leg guard—See guard position.

linear movement—Movements that follow the path of a straight line.

low-maintenance tool—Offensive and defensive tools that require the least amount of training and practice to maintain proficiency. Low maintenance tools generally do not require preliminary stretching.

low-line kick—One of the two different classifications of a kick. A kick that is directed to targets below the assailant's waist level. (See high-line kick.)

lock—See joint lock.

M

maneuver—To manipulate into a strategically desired position.

MAP—An acronym that stands for moderate, aggressive, passive. MAP provides the practitioner with three possible responses to various grabs, chokes, and holds that occur from a standing position. See aggressive response, moderate response, and passive response.

martial arts—The "arts of war."

masking—The process of concealing your true feelings from your opponent by manipulating and managing your body language.

mechanics—(See body mechanics.)

mental attributes—The various cognitive qualities that enhance your fighting skills.

mental component—One of the three vital components of the CFA system. The mental component includes the cerebral aspects of fighting including the killer instinct, strategic and tactical development, analysis and integration, philosophy, and cognitive development. See physical component and spiritual component.

mesomorph—One of the three somatotypes. A body type classified by a high degree of muscularity and strength. The mesomorph possesses the ideal physique for unarmed combat. See ectomorph and endomorph.

mobility—A combative attribute. The ability to move your body quickly and freely while balanced. See footwork.

moderate response—One of the three possible counters when assaulted by a grab, choke, or hold from a standing position. Moderate response requires you to counter your opponent with a control and restraint (submission hold). See aggressive response and passive response.

modern martial art—A pragmatic combat art that has evolved to meet the demands and characteristics of the present time.

mounted position—A dominant ground-fighting position where a fighter straddles his opponent.

muscular endurance—The muscles' ability to perform the same motion or task repeatedly for a prolonged period of time.

muscular flexibility—The muscles' ability to move through maximum natural ranges.

muscular strength—The maximum force that can be exerted by a particular muscle or muscle group against resistance.

muscular/skeletal conditioning—An element of physical fitness that entails muscular strength, endurance, and flexibility.

N

naked choke—A throat choke executed from the chest to back position. This secure choke is executed with two hands and it can be performed while standing, kneeling, and ground fighting with the opponent.

neck crush – A powerful pain compliance technique used when the adversary buries his head in your chest to avoid being razed.

neutralize—See incapacitate.

neutral zone—The distance outside the kicking range at which neither the practitioner nor the assailant can touch the other.

nonaggressive physiology—Strategic body language used prior to initiating a first strike.

nontelegraphic movement—Body mechanics or movements that do not inform an assailant of your intentions.

nuclear ground-fighting tools—Specific grappling range tools designed to inflict immediate and irreversible damage. Nuclear tools and tactics include biting tactics, tearing tactics, crushing tactics, continuous choking tactics, gouging techniques, raking tactics, and all striking techniques.

O

offense—The armed and unarmed means and methods of attacking a criminal assailant.

offensive flow—Continuous offensive movements (kicks, blows, and strikes) with unbroken continuity that ultimately neutralize or terminate the opponent. See compound attack.

offensive reaction time—The elapsed time between target selection and target impaction.

one-mindedness—A state of deep concentration wherein you are free from all distractions (internal and external).

ostrich defense—One of the biggest mistakes one can make when defending against an opponent. This is when the practitioner looks away from that which he fears (punches, kicks, and strikes). His mentality is, "If I can't see it, it can't hurt me."

P

pain tolerance—Your ability to physically and psychologically withstand pain.

panic—The second stage of fear; overpowering fear. See fright and terror.

parry—A defensive technique: a quick, forceful slap that redirects an assailant's linear attack. There are two types of parries: horizontal and vertical.

passive response—One of the three possible counters when

assaulted by a grab, choke, or hold from a standing position. Passive response requires you to nullify the assault without injuring your adversary. See aggressive response and moderate response.

patience—A combative attribute. The ability to endure and tolerate difficulty.

perception—Interpretation of vital information acquired from your senses when faced with a potentially threatening situation.

philosophical resolution—The act of analyzing and answering various questions concerning the use of violence in defense of yourself and others.

philosophy—One of the five aspects of CFA's mental component. A deep state of introspection whereby you methodically resolve critical questions concerning the use of force in defense of yourself or others.

physical attributes—The numerous physical qualities that enhance your combative skills and abilities.

physical component—One of the three vital components of the CFA system. The physical component includes the physical aspects of fighting, such as physical fitness, weapon/technique mastery, and combative attributes. See mental component and spiritual component.

physical conditioning—See combative fitness.

physical fitness—See combative fitness.

positional asphyxia—The arrangement, placement, or positioning of your opponent's body in such a way as to interrupt your breathing and cause unconsciousness or possibly death.

positioning—The spatial relationship of the assailant to the assailed person in terms of target exposure, escape, angle of attack, and various other strategic considerations.

postal attack - see going postal.

power—A physical attribute of armed and unarmed combat. The amount of force you can generate when striking an anatomical target.

power generators—Specific points on your body that generate impact power. There are three anatomical power generators: shoulders, hips, and feet.

precision—See accuracy.

preemptive strike—See first strike.

premise—An axiom, concept, rule, or any other valid reason to modify or go beyond that which has been established.

preparedness—A state of being ready for combat. There are three components of preparedness: affective preparedness, cognitive preparedness, and psychomotor preparedness.

probable reaction dynamics - The opponent's anticipated or predicted movements or actions during both armed and unarmed combat.

proficiency training—A CFA training methodology requiring the practitioner to execute a specific body weapon, technique, maneuver, or tactic over and over for a prescribed number of repetitions. See conditioning training and street training.

progressive indirect attack (PIA) – One of the five methods of attack. A progressive method of attack whereby the initial tool or technique is designed to set the opponent up for follow-up blows.

proxemics—The study of the nature and effect of man's personal space.

proximity—The ability to maintain a strategically safe distance from a threatening individual.

pseudospeciation—A combative attribute. The tendency to assign subhuman and inferior qualities to a threatening assailant.

psychological conditioning—The process of conditioning the mind for the horrors and rigors of real combat.

psychomotor preparedness—One of the three components of preparedness. Psychomotor preparedness means possessing all of the physical skills and attributes necessary to defeat a formidable adversary. See affective preparedness and cognitive preparedness.

punch—A quick, forceful strike of the fists.

punching range—One of the three ranges of unarmed combat. Punching range is the mid range of unarmed combat from which the fighter uses his hands to strike his assailant. See kicking range and grappling range.

punching-range tools—The various body weapons that are employed in the punching range of unarmed combat, including finger jabs, palm-heel strikes, rear cross, knife-hand strikes, horizontal and shovel hooks, uppercuts, and hammer-fist strikes. See grappling-range tools and kicking-range tools.

Q

qualities of combat—See attributes of combat.

quarter beat - One of the four beat classifications of the Widow Maker Program. Quarter beat strikes never break contact with the assailant's face. Quarter beat strikes are primarily responsible for creating the psychological panic and trauma when Razing.

R

range—The spatial relationship between a fighter and a threatening assailant.

range deficiency—The inability to effectively fight and defend in all ranges of combat (armed and unarmed).

range manipulation—A combative attribute. The strategic manipulation of combat ranges.

range proficiency—A combative attribute. The ability to effectively fight and defend in all ranges of combat (armed and unarmed).

ranges of engagement—See combat ranges.

ranges of unarmed combat—The three distances (kicking range, punching range, and grappling range) a fighter might physically engage with an assailant while involved in unarmed combat.

raze – To level, demolish or obliterate.

razer – One who performs the Razing methodology.

razing – The second phase of the Widow Maker Program. A series of vicious close quarter techniques designed to physically and psychologically extirpate a criminal attacker.

razing amplifier - a technique, tactic or procedure that magnifies the destructiveness of your razing technique.

reaction dynamics—see probable reaction dynamics.

reaction time—The elapsed time between a stimulus and the response to that particular stimulus. See offensive reaction time and defensive reaction time.

rear cross—A straight punch delivered from the rear hand that crosses from right to left (if in a left stance) or left to right (if in a right stance).

rear side—The side of the body furthest from the assailant. See lead side.

reasonable force—That degree of force which is not excessive for a particular event and which is appropriate in protecting yourself or others.

refinement—The strategic and methodical process of improving or perfecting.

relocation principle—Also known as relocating, this is a street-fighting tactic that requires you to immediately move to a new location (usually by flanking your adversary) after delivering a compound attack.

repetition—Performing a single movement, exercise, strike, or action continuously for a specific period.

research—A scientific investigation or inquiry.

rhythm—Movements characterized by the natural ebb and flow of related elements.

ritual-oriented training—Formalized training that is conducted without intrinsic purpose. See combat-oriented training and sport-oriented training.

S

safety—One of the three criteria for a CFA body weapon, technique, maneuver, or tactic. It means that the tool, technique, maneuver or tactic provides the least amount of danger and risk for the practitioner. See efficiency and effectiveness.

scissors hold—See guard position.

scorching – Quickly and inconspicuously applying oleoresin capsicum (hot pepper extract) on your fingertips and then razing your adversary.

self-awareness—One of the three categories of CFA awareness. Knowing and understanding yourself. This includes aspects of yourself which may provoke criminal violence and which will promote a proper and strong reaction to an attack. See criminal awareness and situational awareness.

self-confidence—Having trust and faith in yourself.

self-enlightenment—The state of knowing your capabilities, limitations, character traits, feelings, general attributes, and motivations. See self-awareness.

set—A term used to describe a grouping of repetitions.

shadow fighting—A CFA training exercise used to develop and refine your tools, techniques, and attributes of armed and unarmed combat.

sharking – A counter attack technique that is used when your adversary grabs your razing hand.

shielding wedge - a defensive maneuver used to counter an unarmed postal attack.

simple direct attack (SDA) – One of the five methods of attack. A method of attack whereby the practitioner delivers a solitary offenses tool or technique. It may involve a series of discrete probes or one swift, powerful strike aimed at terminating the encounter.

situational awareness—One of the three categories of CFA awareness. A state of being totally alert to your immediate surroundings, including people, places, objects, and actions. (See criminal awareness and self-awareness.)

skeletal alignment—The proper alignment or arrangement of your body. Skeletal alignment maximizes the structural integrity of striking tools.

skills—One of the three factors that determine who will win a street fight. Skills refers to psychomotor proficiency with the tools and techniques of combat. See Attitude and Knowledge.

slipping—A defensive maneuver that permits you to avoid an assailant's linear blow without stepping out of range. Slipping can be accomplished by quickly snapping the head and upper torso sideways (right or left) to avoid the blow.

snap back—A defensive maneuver that permits you to avoid an assailant's linear and circular blows without stepping out of range. The snap back can be accomplished by quickly snapping the head backward to avoid the assailant's blow.

somatotypes—A method of classifying human body types or builds into three different categories: endomorph, mesomorph, and ectomorph. See endomorph, mesomorph, and ectomorph.

sparring—A training exercise where two or more fighters fight each other while wearing protective equipment.

speed—A physical attribute of armed and unarmed combat. The rate or a measure of the rapid rate of motion.

spiritual component—One of the three vital components of the CFA system. The spiritual component includes the metaphysical issues and aspects of existence. See physical component and mental component.

sport-oriented training—Training that is geared for competition and governed by a set of rules. See combat-oriented training and ritual-oriented training.

sprawling—A grappling technique used to counter a double- or single-leg takedown.

square off—To be face-to-face with a hostile or threatening assailant who is about to attack you.

stance—One of the many strategic postures you assume prior to or during armed or unarmed combat.

stick fighting—Fighting that takes place with either one or two sticks.

strategic positioning—Tactically positioning yourself to either escape, move behind a barrier, or use a makeshift weapon.

strategic/tactical development—One of the five elements of CFA's mental component.

strategy—A carefully planned method of achieving your goal of engaging an assailant under advantageous conditions.

street fight—A spontaneous and violent confrontation between two or more individuals wherein no rules apply.

street fighter—An unorthodox combatant who has no formal training. His combative skills and tactics are usually developed in the street by the process of trial and error.

street training—A CFA training methodology requiring the practitioner to deliver explosive compound attacks for 10 to 20 seconds. See condition ng training and proficiency training.

strength training—The process of developing muscular strength through systematic application of progressive resistance.

striking art—A combat art that relies predominantly on striking techniques to neutralize or terminate a criminal attacker.

striking shield—A rectangular shield constructed of foam and vinyl used to develop power in your kicks, punches, and strikes.

striking tool—A natural body weapon that impacts with the assailant's anatomical target.

strong side—The strongest and most coordinated side of your body.

structure—A definite and organized pattern.

style—The distinct manner in which a fighter executes or performs his combat skills.

stylistic integration—The purposeful and scientific collection of tools and techniques from various disciplines, which are strategically integrated and dramatically altered to meet three essential criteria: efficiency, effectiveness, and combative safety.

submission holds—Also known as control and restraint techniques, many of these locks and holds create sufficient pain to cause the adversary to submit.

system—The unification of principles, philosophies, rules, strategies, methodologies, tools, and techniques of a particular method of combat.

T

tactic—The skill of using the available means to achieve an end.

target awareness—A combative attribute that encompasses five strategic principles: target orientation, target recognition, target selection, target impaction, and target exploitation.

target exploitation—A combative attribute. The strategic maximization of your assailant's reaction dynamics during a fight. Target exploitation can be applied in both armed and unarmed encounters.

target impaction—The successful striking of the appropriate anatomical target.

target orientation—A combative attribute. Having a workable knowledge of the assailant's anatomical targets.

target recognition—The ability to immediately recognize appropriate anatomical targets during an emergency self-defense situation.

target selection—The process of mentally selecting the appropriate anatomical target for your self-defense situation. This is predicated on certain factors, including proper force response, assailant's positioning, and range.

target stare—A form of telegraphing in which you stare at the anatomical target you intend to strike.

target zones—The three areas in which an assailant's anatomical targets are located. (See zone one, zone two and zone three.)

technique—A systematic procedure by which a task is accomplished.

telegraphic cognizance—A combative attribute. The ability to recognize both verbal and non-verbal signs of aggression or assault.

telegraphing—Unintentionally making your intentions known to your adversary.

tempo—The speed or rate at which you speak.

terminate—To kill.

terror—The third stage of fear; defined as overpowering fear. See fright and panic.

timing—A physical and mental attribute of armed and unarmed combat. Your ability to execute a movement at the optimum moment.

tone—The overall quality or character of your voice.

tool—See body weapon.

traditional martial arts—Any martial art that fails to evolve and change to meet the demands and characteristics of its present environment.

traditional style/system—See traditional martial arts.

training drills—The various exercises and drills aimed at perfecting combat skills, attributes, and tactics.

trap and tuck – A counter move technique used when the adversary attempts to raze you during your quarter beat assault.

U

unified mind—A mind free and clear of distractions and focused on the combative situation.

use of force response—A combative attribute. Selecting the appropriate level of force for a particular emergency self-defense situation.

V

viciousness—A combative attribute. The propensity to be extremely violent and destructive often characterized by intense savagery.

violence—The intentional utilization of physical force to coerce, injure, cripple, or kill.

visualization—Also known as mental visualization or mental imagery. The purposeful formation of mental images and scenarios in the mind's eye.

W

warm-up—A series of mild exercises, stretches, and movements designed to prepare you for more intense exercise.

weak side—The weaker and more uncoordinated side of your body.

weapon and technique mastery—A component of CFA's physical component. The kinesthetic and psychomotor development of a weapon or combative technique.

weapon capability—An assailant's ability to use and attack with a particular weapon.

webbing - The first phase of the Widow Maker Program. Webbing is a two hand strike delivered to the assailant's chin. It is called Webbing because your hands resemble a large web that wraps around the enemy's face.

widow maker – One who makes widows by destroying husbands.

widow maker program – A CFA combat program specifically designed to teach the law abiding citizen how to use extreme force when faced with immediate threat of unlawful deadly criminal attack. The Widow Maker program is divided into two phases or methodologies: Webbing and Razing.

Y

yell—A loud and aggressive scream or shout used for various strategic reasons.

Z

zero beat – One of the four beat classifications of the Widow Maker, Feral Fighting and Savage Street Fighting Programs. Zero beat strikes are full pressure techniques applied to a specific target until it completely ruptures. They include gouging, crushing, biting, and choking techniques.

zone one—Anatomical targets related to your senses, including the eyes, temple, nose, chin, and back of neck.

zone three—Anatomical targets related to your mobility, including thighs, knees, shins, and instep.

zone two—Anatomical targets related to your breathing, including front of neck, solar plexus, ribs, and groin.

Speed Boxing Secrets

About Sammy Franco

With over 30 years of experience, Sammy Franco is one of the world's foremost authorities on fighting. Highly regarded as a leading innovator in combat sciences, Mr. Franco was one of the premier pioneers in the field of combat instruction.

Sammy Franco is perhaps best known as the founder and creator of Contemporary Fighting Arts (CFA), a state-of-the-art offensive-based combat system that is specifically designed for real-world self-defense. CFA is a sophisticated and practical system of self-defense, designed specifically to provide efficient and effective methods to avoid, defuse, confront, and neutralize both armed and unarmed attackers.

Sammy Franco has frequently been featured in martial art magazines, newspapers, and appeared on numerous radio and television programs. Mr. Franco has also authored numerous books, magazine articles, and editorials, and has developed a popular library of instructional videos.

Sammy Franco's experience and credibility in the combat sciences is unequaled. One of his many accomplishments in this field includes the fact that he has earned the ranking of a Law Enforcement Master Instructor, and has designed, implemented, and taught officer survival training to the United States Border Patrol (USBP). He has instructed members of the US Secret Service, Military Special Forces, Washington DC Police Department, Montgomery County, Maryland Deputy Sheriffs, and the US Library of Congress Police. Sammy

Franco is also a member of the prestigious International Law Enforcement Educators and Trainers Association (ILEETA) as well as the American Society of Law Enforcement Trainers (ASLET) and he is listed in the "Who's Who Director of Law Enforcement Instructors."

Sammy Franco is a nationally certified Law Enforcement Instructor in the following curricula: PR-24 Side-Handle Baton, Police Arrest and Control Procedures, Police Personal Weapons Tactics, Police Power Handcuffing Methods, Police Oleoresin Capsicum Aerosol Training (OCAT), Police Weapon Retention and Disarming Methods, Police Edged Weapon Countermeasures and "Use of Force" Assessment and Response Methods.

Mr. Franco holds a Bachelor of Arts degree in Criminal Justice from the University of Maryland. He is a regularly featured speaker at a number of professional conferences and conducts dynamic and enlightening seminars on numerous aspects of self-defense and combat training.

On a personal level, Sammy Franco is an animal lover, who will go to great lengths to assist and rescue animals. Throughout the years, he's rescued everything from turkey vultures to goats. However, his most treasured moments are always spent with his beloved German Shepherd dogs.

For more information about Mr. Franco and his unique Contemporary Fighting Arts system, you can visit his website at: **SammyFranco.com** or follow him on twitter **@RealSammyFranco**

Other Books by Sammy Franco

SPEED BOXING SECRETS
A 21-Day Program to Hitting Faster and Reacting Quicker in Boxing and Mixed Martial Arts

by Sammy Franco

Speed Boxing Secrets: A 21-Day Program to Hitting Faster and Reacting Quicker in Boxing and Mixed Martial Arts is a comprehensive speed acceleration program made for anyone who wants to dramatically improve their fighting speed in a short period of time. When used correctly, this simple speed development program will double your boxing speed in as little as 21 days. 8.5 x 5.5, paperback, photos, illus, 150 pages.

HEAVY BAG TRAINING
For Boxing, Mixed Martial Arts and Self-Defense (Heavy Bag Training Series Book 1)

by Sammy Franco

The heavy bag is one of the oldest and most recognizable pieces of training equipment. It's used by boxers, mixed martial artists, self-defense practitioners, and fitness enthusiasts. Unfortunately, most people don't know how to use the heavy bag correctly. Heavy Bag Training teaches you everything you ever wanted to know about working out on the heavy bag. In this one-of-a-kind book, world-renowned self-defense expert Sammy Franco provides you with the knowledge, skills, and attitude necessary to maximize the training benefits of the bag. 8.5 x 5.5, paperback, photos, illus, 172 pages.

HEAVY BAG COMBINATIONS
The Ultimate Guide to Heavy Bag Punching Combinations (Heavy Bag Training Series Book 2)

by Sammy Franco

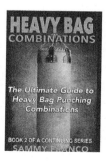

Heavy Bag Combinations is the second book in Sammy Franco's best-selling Heavy Bag Training Series. This unique book is your ultimate guide to mastering devastating heavy bag punching combinations. With over 300+ photographs and detailed step-by-step instructions, Heavy Bag Combinations provides beginner, intermediate and advanced heavy bag workout combinations that will challenge you for the rest of your life! In fact, even the most experienced athlete will advance his fighting skills to the next level and beyond. 8.5 x 5.5, paperback, photos, illus, 248 pages.

HEAVY BAG WORKOUTS
A Hard-Core Guide to Heavy Bag Workout Routines
(Heavy Bag Training Series Book 3)
by Sammy Franco

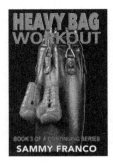

Heavy Bag Workout is the third book in Sammy Franco's best-selling Heavy Bag Training Series. This unique book features over two dozen "out of the box" heavy bag workout routines that will maximize your fighting skills for boxing, mixed martial arts, kick boxing, self-defense, and personal fitness. 8.5 x 5.5, paperback, photos, illus, 208 pages.

HEAVY BAG BIBLE
3 Best-Selling Heavy Bag Books In One Massive Collection
(Heavy Bag Training Series Books 1, 2, 3)
by Sammy Franco

In this unprecedented book collection, world-renowned martial arts and self-defense expert, Sammy Franco takes his thirty years of teaching experience and gives you the most authoritative information for mastering the heavy bag. The Heavy Bag Bible includes Franco's three best-selling heavy bag books collected into one huge paperback collection. This massive 530+ page book contains the entire Heavy Bag Training Series, books 1-3. 8.5 x 5.5, paperback, photos, illus, 538 pages.

DOUBLE END BAG WORKOUT
For Boxing, Mixed Martial Arts & Self-Defense
by Sammy Franco

With over 200 detailed photographs, clear illustrations, and easy-to-follow instructions, Double End Bag Workout: For Boxing, Mixed Martial Arts and Self-Defense has everything you need to start training immediately. Double End Bag Workout also has beginner, intermediate and advanced workout routines that improve your speed, timing, accuracy, attack rhythm, and endurance. Whether you're an elite fighter or a complete beginner, this comprehensive book will take your boxing workout to the next level and beyond! 8.5 x 5.5, paperback, photos, illus, 260 pages.

148

THE COMPLETE BODY OPPONENT BAG BOOK
by Sammy Franco

In this one-of-a-kind book, Sammy Franco teaches you the many hidden training features of the body opponent bag that will improve your fighting skills and boost your conditioning. 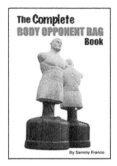 With detailed photographs, step-by-step instructions, and dozens of unique workout routines, The Complete Body Opponent Bag Book is the authoritative resource for mastering this lifelike punching bag. It covers stances, punching, kicking, grappling techniques, mobility and footwork, targets, fighting ranges, training gear, time based workouts, punching and kicking combinations, weapons training, grappling drills, ground fighting, and dozens of workouts. 8.5 x 5.5, paperback, 139 photos, illustrations, 206 pages.

KNOCKOUT
The Ultimate Guide to Sucker Punching
by Sammy Franco

Knockout is a one-of-a-kind book designed to teach you the lost art and science of sucker punching for real-world self-defense situations.  With over 150 detailed photographs, 244 pages and dozens of easy-to-follow instructions, Knockout has everything you need to master the devastating art of sucker punching. Whether you are a beginner or advanced, student or teacher, Knockout teaches you brutally effective skills, battle-tested techniques, and proven strategies to get you home alive and in one piece. 8.5 x 5.5, paperback, 244 pages.

MAXIMUM DAMAGE
Hidden Secrets Behind Brutal Fighting Combination
by Sammy Franco

Maximum Damage teaches you the quickest ways to beat your opponent in the street by exploiting his physical and psychological reactions in a fight. Learn how to stay two steps ahead of your adversary by knowing exactly how he will react to your strikes before they are delivered.  In this unique book, reality based self-defense expert Sammy Franco reveals his unique Probable Reaction Dynamic (PRD) fighting method. Probable reaction dynamics are both a scientific and comprehensive offensive strategy based on the positional theory of combat. Regardless of your style of fighting, PRD training will help you overpower your opponent by seamlessly integrating your strikes into brutal fighting combinations that are fast, ferocious and final! 8.5 x 5.5, paperback, 240 photos, illustrations, 238 pages.

FIRST STRIKE
End a Fight in Ten Seconds or Less!
by Sammy Franco

Learn how to stop any attack before it starts by mastering the art of the preemptive strike. First Strike gives you an easy-to-learn yet highly effective self-defense game plan for handling violent close-quarter combat encounters. First Strike will teach you instinctive, practical and realistic self-defense techniques that will drop any criminal attacker to the floor with one punishing blow. By reading this book and by practicing, you will learn the hard-hitting skills necessary to execute a punishing first strike and ultimately prevail in a self-defense situation. 8.5 x 5.5, paperback, photos, illustrations, 202 pages.

THE BIGGER THEY ARE, THE HARDER THEY FALL
How to Fight a Bigger and Stronger Opponent
by Sammy Franco

Sammy Franco was concerned that no book on the market successfully tackled the specific problem of fighting a larger, stronger opponent. In The Bigger They Are, The Harder They Fall, he addresses that all-important issue and delivers the solid information you'll need to win a street fight when the odds seem stacked against you. In this one-of-a-kind book, Sammy Franco prepares you both mentally and physically for the fight of your life. Unless you're a lineman for the NFL, there may come a day when you will face an opponent who can dominate you through sheer mass and power. Read and study this book before that day comes. 8.5 x 5.5, paperback, photos, illus, 212 pages.

CONTEMPORARY FIGHTING ARTS, LLC
"Real World Self-Defense Since 1989"
www.SammyFranco.com